The Life & Times of the
Brunswick, Bloomsbury

Clare Melhuish

Occasional paper No.5
© Camden History Society   2006

ISBN 0 904491 67 6

Frequently photographed
perspective through the
A-frame structure supporting
the east side of the Brunswick.

The Life & Times of the
Brunswick, Bloomsbury

Clare Melhuish

Occasional paper No.5
of the Camden History Society

Edited by F Peter Woodford
Designed by Ivor Kamlish

Acknowledgements

I would like to thank the residents of the Brunswick and everybody else who has given up time to talk to me about the building and their experience of living there during the course of my research. In particular Stuart Tappin, chairman of the Tenants and Residents' Association, and Isabelle Chaise, have provided invaluable help and support.

This Occasional Paper of the Camden History Society presents part of a doctoral research project supported by Buckinghamshire Chilterns University College (Faculty of Design) and the Arts and Humanities Research Council. I am extremely grateful to Camden History Society and Dr Peter Woodford for giving me the opportunity to publish some of this work, and providing so much valuable editorial support and feedback. Thanks are also due to Ivor Kamlish for his work on the design.

I am indebted to my academic supervisors Dr Greg Votolato and Dr Eric Hirsch for their continuing advice and criticism across the disciplinary boundaries of design and anthropology. I also thank Susannah Stone, my friend and collaborator, for joining me 'in the field' as photographer. Above all, I must thank Patrick Hodgkinson for the many hours of stimulating and enjoyable conversation we have had about the Brunswick.

Finally, I want to thank my husband and sons, Pierre, Ivan and Reynard d'Avoine, for sharing and supporting my interest and work. I wish to dedicate this volume to my late father, Nigel Melhuish, who has sadly missed its publication, and my mother Susan.

For the provision of images and in some cases permission to reproduce them, I wish to thank Patrick Hodgkinson and the Architectural Review; Camden Local Studies and Archives Centre; photographers Susannah Stone and Ivor Kamlish; Richard Einzig/Arcaid; publishers Secker & Warburg and the former Architectural Press, London; the RIBA Drawings Collection at the Victoria and Albert Museum; and architects David Rock, Hawkins/Brown, Squire and Partners, and Levitt Bernstein Associates.

Contents

List of illustrations

Chapter 1

Chapter 2

1 A brief history of the Brunswick

Illustrations numbered in square brackets are shown on pp 75 ff.

In 1967 Mr Spencer, Deputy Town Clerk, heralding the launch of full-scale construction works at the Foundling Estate, subsequently known as the Brunswick Centre, and five years before they came to a premature halt, declared

> "It will bring back, into this central part of London, ordinary family life – in fact, it is what you might call a fist of family life thrust into this area of institutions, offices, hotels and student hostels."

Mr Spencer is quoted in an article for the *Evening Standard* [1] written by one Michael Barsley, a resident of Marchmont Street, which bordered the vast redevelopment site. Offering a contrasting assessment of the Brunswick at that time, Barsley wrote

> "The Marchmont Street area is still full of charm and character – which is why I like to live there, above a butcher's shop ([1], p 75) where, nearly 100 years ago, there was a donkey in the basement, turning a wheel to make the sausage-meat."

In 2006 there is no butcher's shop, and certainly no donkey, in Marchmont Street, but some of the houses built there by James Burton in the early 1800s remain. However, by the 1960s the condition of most of them was as bad as those on the west side of Brunswick Square [2]. The extent of the clearance that took place to make way for the Brunswick Centre [3] was dramatic: three-and-a-half city blocks, from Bernard Street in the south to Handel Street in the north, and from Hunter Street/Brunswick Square on the east to Marchmont Street on the west, entailing the loss of much of Kenton Street and Coram Street. And that was only a truncated version of the originally planned scheme, which would have covered another whole block to the north, taking the bold intervention right up to Tavistock Place on its northern boundary. Demolition and rebuilding on such a scale in the historic centre of London has today become virtually unthinkable.

Local planning policy in the 1960s recognised a creeping institution-alisation of the area, manifested in large faceless building blocks inserted into the historic fabric of small-scale Georgian terraces and squares, and attempted to promote buildings that would support family life to counter that effect. In this book we ask whether the granting of permission for further demolition of that historic fabric to make way for the construction of a major new housing complex, designed on a gigantic scale, has achieved that aim during the building's first 30 years of life. Further, we consider how life in and around the Brunswick may be reshaped by the refurbishment programme started, after many years of controversy and conflict, by freeholder Allied London in February 2005. It was Allied London who, at the suggestion of architect Patrick Hodgkinson, finally dropped the word 'Centre' from the name in 2001. Hodgkinson had always objected to the term as 'an American import of the 1960s', which he never liked. Accordingly, we use the new name, 'the Brunswick' to describe the complex in what follows.

1 Barsley, Michael (1967) 'The Changing Face of Bloomsbury'. *Evening Standard* 3 May, p 8.

The mixed-use development first known as the Foundling Estate, after the nearby Foundling Hospital established by Thomas Coram, comprises two parallel blocks, Foundling Court on Marchmont Street and O'Donnell Court on Brunswick Square. They face each other across what was an open-ended shopping precinct slightly elevated above ground level, to accommodate a double layer of car parking and service access underneath. With nearly 400 flats, the Brunswick is larger than many other local estates, but it is spatially compact, partly because of the way the precinct forges a direct relationship between the two linear blocks, but mainly because, as one resident puts it, *"it doesn't shoot up into the air"* [2]. This effectively sums up the design approach pursued by architect Patrick Hodgkinson, who was resolutely committed to the concept of low-rise, high-density residential development. This was the primary driving force behind the scheme, and its significance in running counter to dominant trends favouring high-rise buildings was highlighted for the general public in Jill Craigie's BBC film *Who are the Vandals?* of 1967. While Craigie singled out the high-rise Regent's Park Estate for particular criticism, high-rise towers were rising all over London during that period, exemplified by the LCC's now iconic Alton Estate, designed by the man who, paradoxically, was to become Hodgkinson's mentor and employer, Sir Leslie Martin.

When asked how they might describe the Brunswick to someone who didn't know it, current residents use a variety of images, but mostly along the same lines: *"I say it is a large building with lots of sloping glass and lots of concrete, and you either think it's a concrete jungle, or...a cruise ship"*, says one. *"Well, it's the one with the ziggurat structure...the greenhouses"*, says another. The most striking visual characteristic of the development, apart from its sheer scale and vast expanse of exposed concrete (now, finally, concealed and protected under a paint finish as originally intended) is the view of cascading glass terraces on both sides of each block – the famous "winter gardens" to the flats which glint in the light on a bright day, and give a view of the sky from within [4]. They were made possible by the use of monolithic concrete A-frame structures for the two housing blocks, rising up seven floors, with the potential for additional floors on top.

The housing blocks are accessible to residents both from the precinct and from the street, where four entrances punctuate the 300-metre-long façades, and articulate the three bays of the construction. The precinct itself, with its shops, restaurants and cinema, has now been closed to the north, but was historically a permeable space of free public access, with open north and south ends, and lateral access from east and west, through the housing blocks. On the east, facing Brunswick Square, a monumental porticoed entrance originally framed a dramatic view [5] of the grand civic staircase, now lost[3], that led up to terrace level within the precinct, while a more modest covered passage on the west forms a small arcade of shops connecting the Brunswick precinct to Marchmont Street (Coram Arcade).

<hr>

2 All quoted comments by residents are from interviews carried out by the author 2001-2006.
3 The original staircase, which was demolished in 2001 for security reasons, is revealed in all its glory in Michelangelo Antonioni's film *The Passenger*, finally re-released in 2006 after years of legal wrangling.

Strangely enough, in view of the Deputy Town Clerk's explicit statement as to the intention to support and promote family life in the area, numerous misconceptions about the building's purpose persist. A former estate manager stated unequivocally that it was built to accommodate 'business people', a notion corroborated by a resident who believes that *"originally [the flats] were designed for people who just worked in London and went home for weekends"*. Someone else says it was designed as 'holiday flatlets', and the Site Superintendent avers that it is *"unfortunately not family-orientated, there's no structure for family life...it was always sort of bedsit land"*. Yet among the longest-standing residents there are some who moved in as a family and remained there as such. For instance, one mother who moved in when she was pregnant and brought up her sons on the estate claims *"at the beginning everyone knew each other... the people who lived in the [nearby] houses before had the option to move in there"*. Many of her new neighbours had known her as a child. Another older lady, who lived on the local Peabody estate when the Brunswick was being built, says she wanted to see what the new flats were like. When she moved in she knew lots of people: *"We'd have cups of tea round each others' flats"*.

Thus, contrary to popular belief, the Brunswick did not represent a complete rupture with the local community; in fact, there was a good deal of local interest in the project and some goodwill towards it. Even so, the clearance of swathes of existing housing to make way for a building which, according to the *Observer Magazine*[4], made "the Georgian streets nearby look like vulnerable dolls' houses", was undoubtedly traumatic. In 1959, when the scheme was first mooted, there was an "immediate outcry from local residents" [5], and a special tenants' and residents' association was formed to fight the scheme. On 31 August 1962, *The Guardian* reported in its 'London Letter: the Future of Bloomsbury', that the future was uncertain for what it described as a 'deeply-rooted' population, including many of modest incomes and many shopkeepers, who *"are not impressed by the prospect of smart new flats, which many will not be able to afford."* Three years later, the same paper published a poignant photograph of a single building awaiting demolition left on the corner of Coram Street, against the bleak backdrop of the huge cleared site. The accompanying story described the displacement of 'hundreds of tenants in houses, shops, hotels and hostels', with particular focus on the 'dispossessed doctors and dentists [who] must find their own accommodation'.

When the *Evening Standard* ran its 1967 story on the changing face of Bloomsbury, it used the same photograph. By that time, the inhabitants of what had become known by the architects as 'the House of Grace and Favour', namely Mr Townsley, a resident of 30 years' standing, and the Raaman family – father, mother and daughter – had been living in this strange situation for more than three years. They are reported by the paper as saying 'We have heard nothing, and all the alternatives have been

---

4 Kendall, Ena (1973) 'Babylon comes to Bloomsbury'. *Observer Magazine*, 2 Dec, p 33.
5 Reported in *North London Press*, 4 June 1965, 'New £10m Foundling Estate plan'.

unsuitable, so here we stay.' During that period, Camden's committee had been actively promoting the scheme, described by chairman Mrs Peggy Duff as *"a very nice development which will improve the area."*[5] But feelings were running high. In 1965 it was also reported that a stormy debate had taken place at a meeting of the Council, in which the redevelopment proposals were attacked. Councillor John Diamond accused property companies of buying up land to develop it purely for profit, without regard for the needs of the people, and Councillor Tucker said there was great anxiety in the area and people were being driven to despair.[6]

History of the site and the developer's concept

By this point the developer, Alec Coleman (also the man behind the ill-fated Tricorn Centre in Portsmouth), was already running into trouble. He had acquired 14 acres of the Foundling Hospital and Holborn Estates (see [6]] in 1958 at a cost of £1,750,000 for 'retention and future development'.[7] The Foundling Hospital itself had been established in 1739 by Thomas Coram, as London's first home for abandoned children. It stood when built in the midst of Lamb's Conduit Fields ([6], upper left; the site of the future Brunswick development shown as a rectangle). It was demolished in 1926 and the institution moved to the country. But long before that, in the 18th century, the Governors of the Foundling Hospital had taken up the development impetus in this neighbourhood to the east of Southampton Row, following the lead established by the Bedford Estate on the west. In 1788, the Hospital was still an isolated building standing in a rural setting, and when the estate announced its intention to build on the surrounding land, on which, unusually, it held the freehold, there was a public outcry at the prospect of losing more open country. All the same, a feasibility study was commissioned from the architect S P Cockerell, who recommended the formation of Mecklenburgh and Brunswick Squares to the east and west sides of the hospital. His intention was to provide a suitable architectural setting for the hospital, so *"as rather to raise than depress the Character of this Hospital itself as an Object of national Munificence"*, and he also set out the principle that if new urban units were to be created they should contain accommodation for all classes.

The governors forged ahead with the implementation of Cockerell's recommendations, and in 1792 were approached by the builder James Burton. He asked for an option to develop housing around the whole of Brunswick Square, but was initially given only the south side and part of Guilford Street. Nevertheless, he gradually acquired control of most of the western part of the Foundling property, so that by 1802 he had built nearly 600 houses on the estate, including the site of the future Brunswick ([6], upper right and lower left).

Thus, the historic urban fabric of the area was of undeniable architectural interest – although Cockerell's development on Mecklenburgh Square was much grander than Burton's work, and the next wave of construction to the west by Thomas Cubitt, namely Tavistock, Woburn, and Gordon Squares,

---

6 In a newspaper, 30 July 1965 – details unknown as material held in LBC file had been discarded.
7 Hillman, Judy (1965) 'Big Bloomsbury plan out soon'. *Evening Standard*, 14 July.

were all in a style and quality of building superior to anything which had been seen before in the speculative market. Burton's houses 'look like jerrybuilding', wrote Summerson[8] in 1945, and fifteen years later, responding to Alec Coleman's planning application, the LCC's Architect in Charge of Historic Buildings, Alec Eden, wrote in a memorandum to the planning officer that:

> *"The houses on the Foundling Estate reflected the latest architectural fashions, but they remain as somewhat plain Speculators' houses, lacking real distinction in their original form, and many of them are now mutilated... none of the streets is in itself outstandingly well-proportioned....Any special architectural or historic interest attaches to the area as a whole rather than to individual streets or terraces, and, if a Building Preservation Order were to be made on the whole estate, it is most unlikely that the Minister of Housing and Local Government would confirm it."* [9]

Already by 1958, Burton's housing between Brunswick Square and Marchmont Street ([1] and [2]) had been condemned as substandard. The houses had been subdivided into a great number of small dwelling units occupied by low-income households, and were mixed with light industrial activities which typically flourished in yards at the centre of each city block – in this case, Brunswick Mews. Marchmont Street, running through the heart of the site, was a busy shopping street, but the surrounding area was war-scarred, as well as blighted by the increasing encroachment of institutional usage – not only London University, but also the Great Ormond Street and Queen Square hospitals, and the new hotels serving mass-market tourism.

Coleman set up a new company, Marchmont Properties, to deal with the development, which was part-financed by Robert McAlpine & Sons. McAlpines were the pre-eminent building contractors of the period, headed by Sir Edwin McAlpine (knighted for his invention of two portable Mulberry Harbours that ensured the success of D-Day in 1944), with a near monopoly on the nation's construction contracts. McAlpines lent Marchmont Properties £3m interest-free until the completion of the project, representing a significant financial interest that would eventually shape the direction of the development. But at the outset, Coleman took the lead in developing a strategy for the site. He divided it into three main constituents ([6], lower right): the largest part, site A, for housing, shops, and entertainment, with car-parking and provision for deliveries, and two smaller sites B and C to the west designated for commercial offices, a hotel, and a new Territorial Army HQ, with car-parking on B, and future housing on C. In the event, Site C and the northern part of Site A were never touched. The initial plan was founded on a vision of thoroughgoing rationalisation of space that would provide a long pedestrian axis between Euston and King's Cross stations to the north and Holborn to the south, thus opening up Bloomsbury to increased office use integrated with new shopping and housing aimed at the upper end of the market. Coleman's idea was in line with the thinking of the time, significantly shaped by Abercrombie and Forshaw's new Statutory Development Plan of 1951, and Conservative government legislation of 1955, which launched a major slum clearance programme.

---

8 Summerson, John (1945). *Georgian London.* Pleiades, London.
9 W A Eden, Architect in Charge, Historic Buildings: Memorandum to the Planning Officer, LCC, 22 December 195?? (date indecipherable).

Planning policy, party politics[10], and the car

When Clement Attlee formed the first majority Labour Government after the Second World War, public policy was infused with socialist reforming idealism, underpinned by a groundswell of optimism for the brave new world of the future; the implications for the built environment were far-reaching. The construction of new, modern mass housing on a grand scale was central to the government's programme. The New Towns Act was passed in 1946, giving the impetus for the construction of whole new communities on low-density, Garden City principles[11] around the hinterland of the capital. These were intended to house not only those left homeless by the destruction of large swathes of London by the Blitz but also those due to be relocated from the 18th- and 19th-century terraced housing condemned for slum clearance. In 1947 the Town and Country Planning Act ordered the county councils to prepare plans for the redevelopment of their areas, and gave them compulsory purchase powers to facilitate the drive towards reconstruction on modern principles.

In 1951, the Labour government was ousted by the Conservatives, who remained in power until 1964. The County of London Plan was published in the first year of the new Conservative government. It addressed the problem of rehousing in the capital itself by proposing a density of 136 persons per acre (4.5 times Garden City densities), one-third of whom should be accommodated in houses, and 60% in 8- to 10-storey apartment buildings. The 80-ft height limit for residential buildings would be relaxed – though not in Bloomsbury. In the same year, the government pledged to build 300,000 new homes per year, raising housing subsidies for local authority housing from £22 to £35 per home. Local authorities were also given powers to license private contractors in order to achieve increased rates of construction for council housing, and private house building was also encouraged.

From 1956 the Conservative government actively promoted the development of high buildings, offering developers and big builders subsidies worth three times more for a flat in a 15-storey block than for a house[12]. 1953, 1954 and 1959 saw the repeal of Labour's town and country planning legislation, which required development profits to be paid to the state, in order to encourage a free market in development land. In 1957 the Rent Act abolished rent control on 810,000 properties and allowed rent increases for 4.3 million houses still controlled, in the hope of persuading landlords to undertake vital programmes of repair and maintenance.

All in all, the prevailing mind-set showed an overwhelming confidence in the power of rationalisation, large-scale redevelopment, and high-rise construction to regenerate and modernise the city, even in the face

10 Source for political chronology: Chris Cook & John Stevenson, *Longman Companion to Britain since 1945*. Pearson Education Ltd, Harlow.
11 The Garden City movement was founded by Ebenezer Howard in 1898, as a model for spacious, high-quality living and working environments incorporating wide streets and public parks, housing designed on Arts and Crafts principles, and a density of 30 persons per acre. The first was built at Letchworth, Herts. in 1903, followed by Welwyn Garden City in 1919, and the model was also used by philanthropists such as the Cadbury family in their development of the Bournville settlement in Birmingham for their workers, and in early council estates of the 1930s.
12 Source: Peter Hall (1988). *Cities of tomorrow*. Blackwell, Oxford.

of increasing anxiety about the quality of the new building and concern about the impact on the existing social fabric. Objectors described the London skyline as being 'shattered' by high-rise blocks, and lamented the proliferation of office blocks no-one wanted, luxury flats no-one could afford and hotels which were beyond the means of the natives. In 1963, Sir Basil Spence, then President of the RIBA, added his weight to the torrent of disapproval, warning:

> *"The speculators are cornering the limited supply of building land in town and country and holding the community to ransom. The money that should be going into better architecture and higher standards is being taken by people who have contributed nothing to the building process."* [13]

Another problem to confront was the rapidly increasing rate of car ownership and the consequent impact of motor travel on towns and cities. The potential crisis had been highlighted as early as 1924 by the French architect-planner Le Corbusier in his manifesto *Urbanisme (The city of tomorrow)* [14]. In it he recommended radical surgery on the historic fabric of Paris to make way for a new urban model, the Ville Contemporaine, where residential accommodation would be concentrated into large blocks equipped with communal facilities, and through-traffic channelled along fast-flowing one-way highways, with heavy goods traffic underground. The residential blocks would be grouped either into a central, vertical area combined with business, or into 'garden cities' around the periphery for suburban workers. The same problem was discussed by the American Lewis Mumford in his 1938 book *The culture of cities* [15]. In this he proposed the comparable, but different, concept of the mixed-use Superblock [7] revealing the influence of Patrick Geddes and the growing environmental philosophy movement. The model reappeared in his 1961 book *The highway and the city*.

So when in 1963 Professor Colin Buchanan produced his *Traffic in Towns* report for the Ministry of Transport, its recommendations stemmed from earlier thinking. Buchanan's proposal was to create traffic-free 'environmental areas', or residential precincts, surrounded by new highways for fast-moving traffic. He urged that the 'rooms of a town', while needing to be served by roads, are effectively destroyed when roads penetrate and subdivide them. He set out to define those areas and locate the network of roads in the cracks between them, on the basis of the estimated amount of traffic that might be generated by buildings in a particular area.

Later, in 1972, Leslie Martin and Lionel March [16] were to publish their retrospective analysis of the implications of those recommendations for an area like the Foundling Estate – which, by then, Martin had already been involved in redeveloping as the 'Brunswick scheme'. They pointed out that Bloomsbury in 1900 could be described, following the American exponent (Jane Jacobs) of 'organic planning' as 'a complex community' [17] made up of intellectuals clustered around University College and the

13 *The Times*, 15 Feb 1963, Report of RIBA discussion on urban environment.
14 Le Corbusier (1924/1947) *The city of tomorrow and its planning* (translated from the 8th French edition of *Urbanisme* by Frederick Etchells). Architectural Press, London.
15 Lewis Mumford (1938/40) *The culture of cities*. Secker and Warburg, London, Section VIII, *Biotechnic civilisation* image section 28 on Urban Rehabilitation, see fig viii.
16 Martin, Leslie and March, Lionel (1972). *The grid as generator* (Chap 1), in Martin and March, eds., *Urban space and structures*. Cambridge University Press.
17 Citing Jane Jacobs (1961) *The death and life of great American cities*. Random House, New York.

British Museum, plus working people, the Italian community around the Italian hospital, hotels, and shops on Marchmont Street. But by 1961 the balance had altered. Fast-moving traffic on the small-scale street grid had subdivided and damaged the area. Site-by-site residential redevelopment at the required density of 136 persons per acre would entail tall blocks of flats, with additional office accommodation in taller, thicker buildings. The hospitals needed to expand but were hemmed in. Basically, *"the pattern [had] congealed"*. The application of Buchanan's recommendations would have established an extensive road and parking system at ground level, with a deck system for pedestrians elevated above it, and some tall buildings above that to reconstitute built space relocated from ground level. Such a futuristic solution was never to be implemented, but as a result of Buchanan's report Marchmont Street, Hunter Street and Brunswick Square were proposed for road widening as part of a new fast-moving traffic system around the Foundling Estate site.

Although Buchanan's specific recommendations were not announced, or adopted by Camden, until the Brunswick scheme was already well developed, the general principles were already well established and played a crucial part in the way the Brunswick scheme was conceived and evolved – as a complete Superblock on the Mumford model, lying between major traffic arteries, and providing good-quality new housing, a large area of open, public space, and a high proportion of new commercial space.

Coleman's planning applications

Between 1958 and 1960, Alec Coleman made a series of planning applications, using architects Covell and Matthews, for redevelopment of the site with large blocks on a podium. These were rejected by the London County Council. Covell and Matthews' approach typified the ruthless redevelopment mentality of the 1950s, incorporating a 40-storey office block overlooking Brunswick Square, three 20-storey blocks of flats, and some long 5-storey blocks along Marchmont Street to include shops and hostel accommodation for the University of London. The LCC was anxious to preserve the residential status of the neighbourhood, and, on 14 March 1958 had voiced its concerns about the 'displacement of people, disruption of community structure of this area'[18], and the scale of proposed high-rise components. In 1959, Coleman was advised to appoint Leslie Martin, who had recently left his position as chief architect at the LCC, as master planner for the site.

Martin was already familiar with the Bloomsbury context, having been retained as architect by London University for the development of its master plan. He was therefore aware of the series of spinal schemes designed in the early 1930s by Charles Holden for the university along a north-south axis. Holden had proposed a monumental structure of blocks and courtyards, extending along a solid, raised central spine, with services and circulation gathered at the intersections of ribs and spine **[8]**, in short, a 'megastructure'. King George V described the scheme as looking exactly like a battleship, and *Country Life* admired it for its 'strong horizontal character

18 LBC Planning File 217.

[which] will give the mass a distinctly classical basis'[19]. Holden's proposals were only partially achieved, but they reveal the power and influence of the university as an aggrandising institution on the tight-knit urban layout of Bloomsbury, and the strong impulse towards large-scale geometric order in reworking the built environment in the years leading up to the County of London Plan.

Martin–Hodgkinson proposals

Despite Martin's appointment in 1960, a new scheme was again rejected on 23 July 1962 on the grounds that it *"would aggravate congestion … too much non-residential use – contrary to Residential Zoning in the Development Plan"*. On a more positive note the LCC's planning department stated that it was in agreement with the principle of comprehensive redevelopment.[18] In February 1963, an outline plan by Martin and his assistant Patrick Hodgkinson for a mixed-use, low-rise development housing 1800 people in 5-storey linear blocks was approved [9]. As Judy Hillman wrote, two years later,

> *"the ingredients … have been mixed, I understand, to provide a new concept in urban living…. The architect, Mr Patrick Hodgkinson, has managed to double the existing residential population to about 1800 in blocks only five storeys high. This means that the development will retain the traditional Bloomsbury scale."* [7 (p 12)]

The scheme met with the LCC's requirement for housing at a density of 200 people per acre, within the 80-ft height limit[20] retained in Bloomsbury (so that the view of St Paul's cathedral from Primrose Hill not be impeded); approval was granted on condition that residential development would be started before the large non-residential element, and Hodgkinson was subsequently appointed sole architect for Site A.

At this point, the scheme encompassed a broad spectrum of accommodation, including rooftop penthouses: as the architect puts it[21], there were

> *"some 16 different housing types, from luxury to professional on to hostels for young medics and nurses working close by, which would have been a good mix for a central London village."*

The shopping precinct, replete with a glass-roofed market-hall, gold mosaics, and prospective retail tenants including Fortnum & Mason, was to have been very upmarket; a recital hall, commemorating the composer George Frederic Handel (a major benefactor of the Foundling Hospital) was also planned. By 1965, however, McAlpines had taken the project over from Coleman, and it had changed direction. This was a direct result of the election in 1964 of Harold Wilson's Labour government, and new legislation on housing introduced by George Brown as minister of housing. The legislation re-established rent control, in order to put an end to exploitative letting practices, and obliged developers to rehouse or compensate all the original tenants of any site earmarked for redevelopment. Coleman had bought the site on the premise that existing tenants had no rights and could be evicted at

---

19 Cited in Eitan Karol and Finch Allibone (eds). *Charles Holden, architect 1875-1960, catalogue.* E Karol, London, 1988.
20 Listing Branch, Historic Buildings and Area Advisory Committee. The Brunswick Centre, Bernard Street, London: Recommendation for listing, August 1992.
21 PH, letter to author, 22 May 2001.

any time, and suddenly found that he was liable to pay an enormous amount of compensation to get the tenants out.

In 1965 the LCC was replaced by the Greater London Council, and Bloomsbury now found itself part of the London Borough of Camden. At Hodgkinson's suggestion Coleman approached Camden's Housing Department to ask them to take out a 99-year lease on the housing, along with responsibility for the tenants. Hodgkinson had been dealing with Camden's new senior planner, Bruno Schlaffenberg, at the LCC in 1963, and thought that Schlaffenberg might be interested in taking on the housing as a flagship project for the new council – a sort of 'present to Camden'[22]. As the Camden New Journal put it[23] in 2005,

> "Camden was pursuing a policy of progressive urban renewal and [Schlaffenberg's] radical inclinations made him ideal for the senior post in the borough's planning department. He opposed the orthodox thinking of the time – that town planning should be undertaken on a zonal basis. He believed people should be able to live close to their places of work, and disapproved of wholly residential communities such as Hampstead Garden Suburb, the model estate built in 1906 without shops or places of employment."

The mixed-use, city centre development proposed at the Brunswick, on a model not seen since the construction of Dolphin Square in Pimlico in 1935-7 (1200 flats and a complete set of civic amenities designed by architect Gordon Jeeves with engineer Oscar Faber), perfectly embodied Schlaffenberg's vision of urban renewal. The Brunswick's break with zoning principles was far more important than the aesthetics of the new development – as Hodgkinson puts it, it was 'the feel, not the look' which mattered – and the deal with Camden was signed in 1966. At the subsequent Public Inquiry held into the borough's pursuit of a compulsory purchase order on the northern section of Site A (eventually abandoned), the general consensus was that not only did the proposed redevelopment represent a housing gain of 366 people on the site, but also that

> "most of the dwellings in the area were built for a different way of life and to lower standards than are proposed in the new development. There is little space between buildings, resulting in poor daylighting, sunlight and privacy and there is inadequate off-street parking or servicing." [24]

In short, this large-scale piece of urban renewal to provide for a community of about 1,600 people would be a valuable gain to the Holborn area as a whole, especially in the light of mounting concerns about its continuing depopulation – from 70,910 persons in 1891 to 24,810 in 1951, 22,008 in 1961, and 18,482 in 1966. And it was stated in no uncertain terms that an equivalent 'quantity and quality of housing and amenity could not be achieved by piecemeal renewal'.

Changes of direction

The sale of the lease to the council was agreed on the basis that the developer would build a platform over the shopping centre (the terrace, or podium, as it

---

22 PH in conversation with the author, 7 Jun 2000.
23 Obituary of Bruno Schaffenberg, 'Dynamic town planner with an unorthodox vision'. *Camden New Journal*, 10 Feb 2005, p 4.
24 Public Inquiry into LBC Compulsory Purchase Order: Report, 3 Nov 1970.

is now known), allowing the flats to be built separately on top of it, providing a brief history accommodation for at least 1500 people, with a first phase accommodating 700 to be completed by the end of 1967, and all existing protected tenants on the site to be rehoused by the council.[25] At this point, released from the need to borrow money to finance the housing, McAlpines asserted its control over the project. This led inexorably to the removal four years later of both Coleman as chairman of the development company and Coleman's architect, Patrick Hodgkinson, who by then had completed work on all the necessary drawings. By 1970 the scheme itself had also changed in character, chiefly on account of the austerity package introduced by the Labour government in 1966 involving new building controls and cuts in public investment. This meant that the housing had to be redesigned to a lower specification.

The original speculative scheme had been for a broad spectrum of accommodation, encompassing at two ends of the scale penthouse flats on top of the main blocks, and hostel accommodation for nurses and students in the perimeter blocks, with a range of studios to three-bedroom flats in between. Between 1965 and 1968 Hodgkinson redesigned the accommodation, at the council's direction, to provide only standard one- and two-bedroom flats and bedsits and a small number of two-bedroom maisonettes, and lopping off the top floor. The original 18-ft grid (giving the width of the living-room and of the two bedrooms side by side) was also too large to qualify for funding as public housing, and was cut back to a relatively ungenerous 13′6″. The prospective retail tenants lined up by Coleman had disappeared when they heard about the approach to Camden and the redesign of the development as council housing, leaving the whole concept of the shopping precinct much diminished and the way clear for a reduction of the commercial specification on McAlpines' part.

In the meantime, progress was continuing on the commercial redevelopment of Site B under the supervision of a new architect, Ardin and Brookes and Partners, and the general ambition of the project was being scaled down. In 1968, planning permission for an airline passenger terminal on part of the site between Tavistock Place and Bernard Street was refused by the GLC, and in 1971 the government rejected Camden council's bid to make a compulsory purchase order on the site occupied by the Territorial Army HQ on Handel Street, to the north of site A – apparently because ownership of the building could not be definitively established. This was a major setback, meaning that the extension of the Brunswick to Tavistock Place would never be achieved, and the rehousing targets it embodied would never be met. It was reported in *Building Design*, under the ominous headline 'Floundering at the Foundling'[26] that the TA would not accept the offer of alternative accommodation at 16 Chenies Street because the Handel Street building

> *"contains a large gun, which is raised from basement to ground floor by an expensive hydraulic lift. The TA refused to move it... apparently because a war might break out during the process."*

Although no war materialised on the national stage, the council's internal affairs and party politics were rapidly deteriorating into a local civil war, and increasing problems posed by the Brunswick development played no small part in fuelling the conflict.

25 Camden Council press release, 20 Jul 1965.
26 *Building Design*, 14 May 1971.

By July 1971, Phase 1 was nearing completion under the supervision of architects Bikerdike Allen and Rich, whom the council had appointed in 1965, but the following year strong disapproval was voiced regarding the change of use of the non-residential units on the terrace level to professional offices, on the grounds that it was 'contrary to the policy of restricting the growth of office accommodation in the Central Area', and its residential zone status. In 1979 this was rectified by a further change of use to light industrial, providing that the units were used only for suitably quiet activities – engraving, dentistry, optical works, watch repairs, jewellery and typewriter repairs, and nothing else. Meanwhile in 1974, the cancellation of the roof to the shopping mall and the bridge across the mall at terrace level had aroused further disapproval, and from 1973 residents were complaining to the Council about various sources of noise, unbearable heat from the winter gardens, and flooding caused by drainage problems. By 1979 these complaints had become so vociferous that rent reductions were implemented, on the grounds that the building had degenerated into a slum, and for the next 25 years the problems were to rumble on, raising serious questions over the future of the building.

The social context

In 1964, bedsits were considered perfectly respectable accommodation, and a two-bed flat quite adequate for a family with two children, even of different sexes. Tower blocks were the norm, and very few flats were being built with more than two bedrooms. But Hodgkinson claims that "Camden Council turned [the Brunswick] into a ghetto by wanting only 1, 2 and 3-room units." [21 (p 17)] Some authorities allege that there was never any intention of housing families at the Brunswick, and that the flats were made uniformly for childless households from Camden's housing list. 'Our average families would not like living south of the Euston Road', said the Housing Manager to Patrick Hodgkinson, justifying the reduction of space[27]. This seems a curious comment in view of the Council's own policy statements in favour of family life and the continuation of social networks previously existing on the Brunswick site, and can only be understood in the context of the territorial rivalries that the creation of the larger borough councils brought to the surface.

According to June Foskett, the former estate manager of the Brunswick, the range of accommodation there was narrower than in other local estates for which she had responsibility, and failed to serve the interests of families, as had been intended. Those who found it difficult to accommodate their children comfortably were forced to move away, and as a result, an older network of family connections and cohesion has suffered erosion over two generations, even as newer family units from more diverse backgrounds have moved in, both as Council tenants and as leaseholders. We explore this aspect of the Brunswick in Chapter 4.

27 Alan Powers and Stuart Tappin. Notes for a *Bloomsbury Walk* on 14 June 2001. Twentieth Century Society, London.

2 The architect of the Brunswick & his concept

Illustrations numbered in square brackets are shown on pp 82 ff.

When Alec Coleman first approached Leslie Martin to take on the Foundling Estate in 1960, Patrick Hodgkinson had been working in Martin's Cambridge atelier for 3 years, primarily on three schemes: a proposed housing development for St Pancras Borough Council, a new student accommodation building, Harvey Court, for Gonville & Caius College, Cambridge [10], and the St Cross library group in Oxford.

Hodgkinson had been a student at the Architectural Association school (1950-1955) in London, when a project of his for an alternative approach to housing under development by the LCC on a site in Brixton [11] caught Martin's eye. Hodgkinson later wrote of this project:

> *"The LCC's recipe produced a mixed-height development with couples and small families in watered-down Unités, larger families in three-storey blocks and old people in gnomes' bungalows, the worst sort of social segregation. Nothing was in scale or sympathy with surrounding, turn-of-the-century streets which, in the visionaries' minds, would go.*
>
> *My own student project (1953) for the same site achieved a similar density to the LCC scheme, but to the scale of the existing stock, in linear terraces enclosing garden courts. I had taken the Unité 3-floor pack and developed it to suit our climate and habits in a way that produced the social mix of any traditional street."* [1]

Leslie Martin was intrigued by Hodgkinson's low-rise/high-density approach, which they were subsequently to develop in collaboration in a project for St Pancras Borough Council (not actually built). But in 1953 Martin was still working for the LCC, in charge of the very different, high-rise Alton Estate scheme at Roehampton, described in the same article by Hodgkinson as *"that shotgun marriage of Nordic and Corbusian principles whose park setting provided its garden-city image."* The tall housing slabs, clearly visible from nearby Richmond Park and for miles around, would subsequently become iconic symbols of the problems of the new tower-block estates, which by 1968 and with the catastrophic collapse of Ronan Point due to a gas explosion had been almost totally discredited.

By 1968, however, Martin's LCC days were well behind him; he had accepted the first professorship in architecture at the University of Cambridge in 1956, and established his own practice there. By 1968, he and Hodgkinson had also parted company, the latter opening his own office in London to run the Brunswick project as sole architect in 1964. Much later, they were to work together again, but for many years Hodgkinson operated as a sole practitioner, assisted on the Brunswick project by six members of staff: David Levitt, David Bernstein (who were subsequently to form Levitt Bernstein), Anthony Richardson, Peter Myers, Dugald Campbell and chief assistant Chris Hulls.

---

1 Patrick Hodgkinson, 1987. A handful of homes: British post-war housing. A3 Times No.9, *Modern Urban Living*. Polytechnic of North London, pp 19-21.

As Hodgkinson recalls today,

> *"Davids Levitt and Bernstein were responsible for housing, Anthony Richardson and Dugald Campbell for the commercial parts, Peter Myers for external detailing and Christopher Hulls for technical aspects throughout, including site supervision. Previously, Bernstein had worked for Louis Kahn in Philadelphia and Myers for Jorn Utzon in Sidney, on whose advice he came to me. After my resignation Levitt, Bernstein and Richardson opened their own offices in London and Myers his own in Sidney, while Hulls bought a tumbledown timber farmhouse in Hereford, pulled it to bits and rebuilt it with his own hands. Together they had made an ideal design team, for which I have ever been grateful."* [2]

Hodgkinson's background and education

From the moment Hodgkinson decided to enter architectural training, he had a clear sense of direction about the way he hoped to practise architecture, and what it should do in society, notions strengthened by his father's intense opposition to the profession and blank refusal to support his son in it.

As Hodgkinson says, he took up architecture

> *"because it was a profession about people,... caring about people,... humanistic. When I joined the AA in 1950, there was a wonderful future ahead of us... it was all about rebuilding the nation after the war and what we were going to do for people, and those were things that we cared about and very little else."* [3]

Most of his fellow students came from backgrounds very different from his own. They were all 'urban types', as he puts it, whereas he was brought up on farms in Suffolk and Norfolk, and always thought he would farm himself and practise architecture in tandem: *"I was interested in the land, and that was my background...the background that I cared about".* [3] He was sent to school at Charterhouse, leaving at the age of 17 because his father wanted to save on fees, and he was about to be expelled in any case for schoolboy misdemeanours. Hodgkinson had no regrets, not having any great interest in school work, and seeing his departure as an opportunity to return to the countryside and engage with his primary interest. He had, however, spent much of his time at school painting, and after an encounter with local landscape artist Arnesby Brown near his home, he started working with him as an assistant, before deciding, on account of his obsession with painting rocks, that he would become an architect – and 'make' rocks himself, 'full of people'.

Although his two elder sisters were already in London studying music and drama, his father, from a family of northern mill-owners, refused point-blank to pay for Hodgkinson to attend the AA school, or to contribute to his living expenses, making it clear that he would prefer him to join the Stock Exchange. On his mother's side of the family, which hailed from Ireland (his grandfather employed people to collect seaweed around the coast and 'more or less' invented Marmite), there was more of an artistic tradition: she herself was a dancer before her marriage, and she supported Hodgkinson's ambitions. In fact it was through her connections that, after a year's national service, first in the Navy as a stoker and then in the Fleet Air Arm, he joined

---

2 PH, note to author 28.4.06.
3 Author's conversations with PH 2005-6.

the small practice of Ward & Austin, architects and furniture designers based in Villiers Street, Charing Cross. Ward & Austin had designed the shopfront of the Council for Industrial Design in the Haymarket, then headed by Gordon Russell, a furniture designer, and husband of Hodgkinson's mother's sister. Gordon's brother was another furniture designer, a partner in the firm Russell and Gooden, who occupied the same Villiers Street building as Ward & Austin (as did Basil Spence), and designed the wavy-roofed Lion and Unicorn Pavilion at the Festival of Britain.

After a year working at Ward & Austin, Hodgkinson began to study at the AA school, but continued employment by the practice enabled him to pay his way. Ward & Austin were also involved in the Festival of Britain, and Hodgkinson worked with them on the design of the Riverside Restaurant beneath Waterloo Bridge. Hodgkinson loved the Festival, unlike peers of his such as Jim Stirling, who considered it much 'too Swedish', and other critics who disliked its populist character and derided what was called 'People's Detailing'. That agenda fitted in with Hodgkinson's own idea of architecture as a humanist profession as well as an interest in Scandinavian modernism that was to develop through his 1953-4 experience of working for Alvar Aalto in Finland – even though the light, curvy grace of a building such as the Riverside Restaurant may seem remote from his subsequent work.

Hodgkinson considered the AA at that time 'just an art school', although Felix Samuely taught engineering, making maths and geometry 'all suddenly so simple'. When Samuely was working on the American Embassy building with his partner Frank Newby, he employed Hodgkinson to make the axonometric drawings of the complex structure that would explain it to the engineers.

But despite a relaxed and somewhat dilettante atmosphere there was a strong 'cult of Le Corbusier' at the AA which Hodgkinson did not subscribe to. In fact, Frederic Osborn of the Town and Country Planning Association complained about the overpowering influence of the French architect-planner in a letter to Lewis Mumford in 1952.[4] In 1951 Hodgkinson went to Marseilles to see Le Corbusier's Unité d'Habitation [12], the first built example of his innovative prototype for mass housing designed as a concrete slab block raised on stilts. But his personal experience of the Unité convinced him that it was the wrong solution to future housing construction. Le Corbusier's technocratic rationalism was fundamentally at odds with his own vision of architecture, and also with his personal experience of French culture gained through a number of return visits to Paris dating from 1948.

As Hodgkinson recalls, Paris seemed incredibly exciting at that time, after the war. It was ravaged by the conflict, but it *"represented tremendous hope... everything was leaping about...it was really marvellous."* By contrast, *"there was something really rather unpleasant about London – everyone was so proud of having won the war".*[5] Hodgkinson used to go there on the cheap, hitch-hiking at both ends: *"I had no money. You slept under the bridges. It was regally comfortable. I went for the cultural life, the general philosophical discussion that was on at the time".* In the course of these visits, he made friends with the city, and, especially with Juliette Greco, who used to sing in a tiny bar in

4 Frederic Osborn (1952). Letter to Lewis Mumford.
5 PH, in conversation with author 6.10.05.

rue Jacob. He was strongly attracted by existentialist philosophy, as propounded by Sartre, and it was to be a significant influence on his developing attitudes towards architectural practice:

> *"It was simple in those days for the young to sit at the feet of Jean-Paul Sartre at the Café Flore. When I remarked to Sartre that there was nothing existential about [Le Corbusier's] Villa Savoye* **[13]**, *he agreed and directed me across the boulevard to [Pierre Chareau's] Maison de Verre* **[14]**. *From this time, and disagreeing with much that we were then told about the beginnings of European Modernism, I felt strongly that a modern architecture should concern itself with the psyche of the individual rather than being a vehicle for socialism".*[6]

Back at the AA Hodgkinson found inspiration in a range of other sources, especially the architectural traditions of his own country – notably the English Gothic and other medieval building traditions. He loved the English hall tradition represented by

> *"magical great houses like Penshurst, Haddon and Lacock and their smaller, manorial sisters....Born of castles opening their walls to light and of monastic colleges' enlightenment, their lofty great halls the public spaces to which more intimate parlours, solars, chapels and offices attached... these halls seem often like roofed courts."* [1 (p 21)]

By the end of his student years he had also become interested in the 19th-century revival of these traditions, in the work of the 'good' English Arts and Crafts architects, notably Lethaby and Voysey – 'though you couldn't mention that sort of thing to other students. They would have laughed you to scorn.' Thus, while his contemporaries continued to focus on the built and published manifestos of Le Corbusier and the Bauhaus, Hodgkinson made the decision at the end of his third year to leave London and work with Alvar Aalto in Finland for 9 months, even though he had some misgivings about the possibility of turning into 'an Aaltophile'. 'His...work was a very personal poetry, but what I most admired about it was its existentialism, or something close'. In the event, he was tempted to stay in Helsinki to complete his training, but it was Aalto who encouraged him to return to England and 'when he came to Cambridge in 1961 and I showed him Harvey Court, he whistled and confirmed he had been right'.

By that time, Hodgkinson had been working for Leslie Martin for a few years. His contemporaries could not really understand his decision to do so: *"I think my own generation thought it was odd that I was taking a job with him and going to Cambridge with him...because they didn't understand him, they didn't know enough about him"*. The arrival of the Brunswick project in Martin's office sealed Hodgkinson's future. Alec Coleman had seen the unbuilt St Pancras housing scheme published in an issue of *Architectural Design* in 1959, and understood its potential for the Foundling site. He had also been advised to enlist Leslie Martin as a skilful and influential politician, with intimate knowledge of the inner workings of the LCC. On learning that Coleman had formed a partnership with McAlpines, Martin was reluctant to get involved with the project. During his days as Chief Architect at the LCC, he had had his fill of Sir Edwin, who pestered him persistently for new contracts. Martin was happy, however, to set

6 PH, letter to author, 3.9.00.

Hodgkinson to drawing up an alternative to Coleman's rejected slab-block scheme, and a model of the new concept was quickly produced.

Although Hodgkinson was, in his own words, 'a relatively poor reader', and has always stressed his non-academic approach to architecture, he had been reading Lewis Mumford's books, particularly *The culture of cities*[7], in which he describes the concept of the superblock. Mumford seemed to point the way towards a brighter future after the dreadful war years, while his later (1964) book *The highway and the city* offered an overt criticism of the Unité concept, or 'the Marseilles folly', as he put it.[8] Hodgkinson states

> "I can safely say... that Mumford was my largest inspiration.....As for directly architectural influences, I was not drawn by Corbu, Gropius or Mies, more by Futurism than Cubism. I much admired Mendelsohn's German buildings – I thought of him as a Futurist, not an Expressionist, but I was not too impressed by Sant'Elia because he built nothing..." [6]

At that time, in an architectural and planning climate dominated by the ruthless thinking and practice of Le Corbusier and the European school of functionalist Modernism, Hodgkinson's rich mix of influences and referents – English Gothic, Arts and Crafts and the Festival of Britain, from Scandinavian and Modernism to Futurism, and from Sartrian existentialism to Lewis Mumford – was unusual. When it came to relating this eclectic mixture directly to his design work in the late 1950s, Hodgkinson's guiding principle was

> "not to play with an English translation of Le Corbusier's urbanism, as the LCC had done over the summer of that same decade, but to advance a way of building which instead started with the found, and sound, fabric of city".

At the Brunswick, it was

> "about making a new village for central London, rich with the panoply of life of the West End's villages of old yet possessing a new, life-giving spirit." [9]

Hodgkinson was deeply opposed to the *tabula rasa* approach that had underpinned the slum clearance policies of the 1950s, writing of the County of London plan's authors:

> "Sir Patrick Abercrombie with his henchman Forshaw – but without much foresight – was to improve away the life a pre-war London had known... The Foundling Estate presented an opportunity to again bring together living, work and recreation to stimulate each other, against normal practice of the time...it would have been a rich village, rich in gain for everyone living there and using it as well as for its owners....I was told it was a 'bit messy' by an RIBA judge once. I have never believed in modern architecture as 'art', but rather as the craft of making liveable towns and cities. If that craft gives ordinary people their dignity and adds a life-giving sense of spirit, that is enough".[9]

In fact, one of Hodgkinson's criticisms of the Scandinavian tradition of modernism was that 'it made no attempt to create an urban framework',[10]

---

7 Mumford, Lewis (1940) *The culture of cities*. Secker and Warburg, London.
8 Mumford, Lewis (1964) *The highway and the city*. Secker and Warburg, London.
9 PH, Speculation with Humanity?, architect's objection to Tranmac's planning application, 10 July 1992.
10 PH (1972). 'Foundling Conception' *Architectural Review* October, pp 216-217 .

and this was a problem which he sought to address by reference to the work of Lewis Mumford and other American, as opposed to European, sources, particularly the work of the newly-recognised architect Louis Kahn, who in his early 50s had just opened his own practice. But above all, he looked to the native 18th- and 19th-century traditions of English 'town making'. Hodgkinson held the *"strong belief that we could do it again if only we stopped borrowing from abroad".*[11] Furthermore, he saw housing, 'ordinary stock', as a crucial component of this equation: *"housing, after all, is the stuff of which towns are made, rather than public palazzos which only serve to decorate. For myself, to rethread the needle was the task".*

In a sense, then, Hodgkinson, the farmer's son, consciously adopted a role of championing English artistic and cultural traditions, the English landscape and its vernacular building forms, in opposition to the European interests of his metropolitan contemporaries. This passion is reflected in his enduring love of the work of native painters such as Augustus John and William Nicholson. So it is hardly surprising that a point he was always keen to stress about his design for the Brunswick was its engagement with the local context of Georgian terraces. Perhaps it was no coincidence that he subsequently moved (1978) to Bath, one of the most beautiful of Britain's Georgian cities, to take up a post in the architecture school at the university, where he subsequently became Professor of Architecture and head of the Diploma school. As far as he was concerned, the Unité d'Habitation in Marseilles had turned out to be an *'impenetrable slab unacceptable for towns and society...stranded, alien to its surroundings, severing the continuity of space or time.'* He noted that, while tall point blocks exert a radial force on their surroundings, producing 'residual and negative space' (as in Ville Radieuse [15]), linear buildings, exemplified by the Georgian terraces organised in streets, crescents, and squares, have the potential to contain space positively.[10] The Unité model was, he said, essentially unsuitable for transplantation to the English climate, drawing a parallel with the relation between diet and environment:

> *"I have never really forgiven Elizabeth David for trying to teach us to cook Mediterranean food, simply because it does not suit our raw materials or our climate".*[11]

By contrast, the English Georgian model of housing design was eminently suitable to the temperate British climate, supporting high densities of occupation in conjunction with open spaces.

One aspect of that model Hodgkinson did not like was the clear social hierarchy it embodied, visually ordered as the houses were into recognisable classes of dwelling, but Mumford's proposition offered a way of potentially dissolving and reshaping that order into a more egalitarian and socially acceptable model. Thanks to Mumford, then, Hodgkinson fully believed he could re-present at the Brunswick a romantic evocation of a unique, native tradition of construction and settlement patterns, fused with the English landscape and climate which he knew and loved so well. As he put it in 1992, he had envisaged *"a village...overlooking nature...[a] green valley"*[12], and it was a source of considerable chagrin to him that the trees and grass for which planning consent had been obtained were never planted.

---

11 PH, letter to author, 22.5.01.
12 PH (1992) How green, this Bloomsbury valley? Architect's Statement, July.

Neither megastructure nor Le Corbusier

When the Brunswick was finally Listed as a building of historical and architectural importance in 2000, it was described in the Department of Culture, Media and Sport's Listing schedule as

> "a pioneering example of a megastructure in England: of a scheme which combines several functions of equal importance within a single framework. It is also the pioneering example of low-rise, high-density housing, a field in which Britain was extremely influential on this scale....Brunswick developed the concept of the stepped section on a large scale and for a range of facilities, whose formality was pioneering".[13]

This assessment had been preceded by English Heritage's recommendation for listing the building Grade II* in 1992, when it stated that it "admirably fills all the criteria" for a megastructure:

> "It is multi-functional, a 'piece of the city', capable of filling one's needs without having to step outside it, and it is theoretically capable of infinite expansion.....As architectural theory turned into actual building, only the shopping centre at Cumbernauld in Scotland [see [30], p 89] can compete, and that has been much more heavily altered." [14]

In 1993, EH's London Advisory Committee, responding to a planning application to make alterations to the building, described the Centre as a *"multi-functional 'megastructure'...monolithic in its architectural form, the concrete of which it is built reinforcing the expansive scale of the structure"*[15] The UK branch, International Working Party for Documentation and Conservation of Buildings, Sites and Neighbourhoods of the Modern Movement (DOCOMOMO UK) endorsed the Ministry's assessment of the building's significance as a megastructure in March 2000, but also – and somewhat controversially – opposed its Listing, by proposing an expanded definition of the megastructure concept as a framework that accepts and assumes change within it over time.

The Brunswick was dubbed a megastructure by the architecture critic Reyner Banham in his book of 1976[16], following Theo Crosby's analysis[17] in the *Architectural Review*'s special celebratory issue on the Brunswick of October 1972. Crosby had described the Brunswick as

> "...perhaps the first built example of the idea of the urban 'megastructure' – a building that is a city, rather than being merely a component in a city."

His appraisal was mostly complimentary, as was that of Banham, who described the building as *"The most pondered, most learned, most acclaimed, most monumental, most bedevilled in its building history of all English megastructures – and seemingly the best-liked by its inhabitants."*[16]

13 Department for Culture, Media and Sport. Listing Schedule 798-1/95/10155: Brunswick Square (west side), 2000.

14 Harwood, Elain (1992) *The Brunswick Centre (Foundling Estate)*. Report for English Heritage in support of listing, August 1992, updated and revised January 2000, p 7.

15 Croad, Zoe (1993) *The Brunswick Centre*. Report for English Heritage: London Advisory Committee, 5.11.1993, p 1.

16 Banham, Reyner (1976). *Megastructure: urban futures of the recent past*. Thames & Hudson, London, pp 185-189.

17 Crosby, Theo (1972). Brunswick Centre, Bloomsbury, London. *Architectural Review* Vol 152 No. 908 (October) p 211.

For Hodgkinson, however, the use of the term *megastructure* has never been a compliment, and it bears no relation to what he had intended in the design of the Brunswick. For one thing, Banham traced the history of megastructures back to another scheme by Hodgkinson's bugbear, Le Corbusier – the relentlessly rationalising, aggrandising Fort l'Empereur ([27], p 88) designed for Algiers in 1931. As Hodgkinson says, his last two years at the AA had been blighted by his resistance to the cult of Le Corbusier that reigned there, as a result of which he got very little work done. In contrast to Banham, Hodgkinson's friend the critic Colin Rowe described the megastructure, in an unpublished essay[18] on the Brunswick of 1971, as *"originating as a protest against the urbanistic platitudes of Le Corbusier, Ludwig Hilbersheimer, Walter Gropius et al."*, but pointed out that *"[it] has ...become a symbol of authoritarian imposition"*. The idea of the Brunswick as a megastructure is and always has been completely unpalatable to Hodgkinson, whose concept always was to realise a dream of social idealism and equality in an architectural form conceived not as homage but as spirited riposte to Le Corbusier and his followers.

Hodgkinson saw the Brunswick as the direct descendant of a much older, native model of urban form – the Adelphi, designed and built as a grand speculative development of houses over vaulted warehouses by the Adam brothers from 1768. The Brunswick was the first London development since the war to mix housing with other uses and, like the Adelphi, it represented a fusion of speculation on a grand scale with ambitious architectural vision and enormous risk. Interestingly enough, Steen Eiler Rasmussen, in his discussion of the Adelphi, suggests[19] that *"This creative speculation is something very English, and it is no less typical that when it turns out a failure* [as it did at the Adelphi – the warehouses remained vacant, and the houses were not popular], *the enterprise is saved by a lottery..."*. Rasmussen reminds us that *"at the time when [the Adelphi] was built it was very imposing and was by contemporaries considered to represent the very idea of the great modern city."*

Hodgkinson's vision of the Brunswick, like the Adelphi, was driven by a forward-looking desire to realise an idealistic vision of the modern city – in that sense, Hodgkinson had more in common with Le Corbusier than he might want to recognise. He acknowledges that one of his sources of inspiration was Jean Cocteau's film, *La vie commence demain* (*Life begins tomorrow*), an artistic statement about a visionary future which features, amongst others, Le Corbusier at the Unité d'Habitation in Marseilles. One of the metaphors he used to describe the Brunswick was that of the ocean liner, made famous by Le Corbusier as an embodiment of 'a beauty of a more technical order' which would be the foundation of the 'new architecture' described in his manifesto of the same name[20]. For Hodgkinson, the significance of the liner metaphor was distinct from that evoked by Le Corbusier. It was all about social structure and identity, rather than aesthetics – the Brunswick as *"a liner without class distinctions on its promenade decks"*, not an embodiment of innovative architectural form-making. Hodgkinson has always staunchly maintained that the Brunswick is not modern at all. In fact, he saw the Brunswick in the simplest, most

18 Rowe, Colin (1971). 'A Palais Royale for London?', unpublished essay. Ithaca, NY.
19 Rasmussen, Steen Eiler (1934/1982). *London: the unique city*. MIT Press, Cambridge, Mass. pp 179-187.
20 Le Corbusier (1923). 'Eyes Which Do Not See', in *Towards a new architecture* (*Vers une architecture*, trans. Frederick Etchells). Architectural Press, London.

traditional terms as 'a glass-covered market hall' – not subsequently built – and 'a long quiet square with gravel and trees'.[1] (p 21)   *original concept*

Not quite Futurist either

But for many amongst critics and the public alike, the Brunswick was, and remains, indubitably modern – all the more so today, when the clock has turned back so decisively on architectural innovation in the public realm, and the days of experiments like the Brunswick are over. It was the asymmetrical, concrete A-frame section carrying the housing on each side of the precinct that seemed to focus people's attention: as Reyner Banham succinctly wrote, *"by purely visual criteria...it obviously looks like a megastructure"*.[16] (p 27) And megastructures were equated with modernity. Banham went further in endorsing the project's ultra-modern credentials, insisting that the scheme owed much to the work of the Italian Futurist architect Sant'Elia who, in his Manifesto of 1914, had famously rubbished traditional architecture, exalting 'the new beauty of cement and steel' in architecture, the construction of a futurist city modelled on 'an immense, bustling shipyard', with 'metallic catwalks and high-speed conveyor belts', and the futurist house as 'a kind of gigantic machine'[21]. Banham described Sant'Elia as "the virtual inventor of both the A-frame Terrassenhäuser section and the vision of giant buildings spanning over traffic arteries" and the Brunswick as a tribute to him, as:

> *"one of the ultimate ancestors of megastructure....Not only do the residential sections, with their 'case a gradinate' over tall public access spaces within the A-frames proclaim his paternity; so also do the twinned towers flanking the entrances and stairs, the modelling and the battering of the surfaces around those entrances...".*

But Sant'Elia's mechanical, inhumane vision of architecture and the city, which celebrated brutality and ugliness, could not have been more opposed to Hodgkinson's English pastoral inclinations.

When English Heritage in its 1992 Listing appraisal of the Brunswick again highlighted a Sant'Elia connection, suggesting that the grand portico to Brunswick Square in particular was 'a direct crib' from Sant'Elia's Milan railway station project [16], Hodgkinson was at pains to disassociate himself from it, explaining that he didn't even know the project at the time he was designing the Brunswick.[6] (p 24) Indeed, he always refers to his own 'portico' at the Brunswick as a 'loggia', which originated as an integral part of a classically-inspired 'cornice' running the length of the building above the housing terraces [17]. This linear feature, with the appearance of an arcade, was conceived to balance the strip of ventilation slots running along the base of the building, and was an element of the original planning consent that was never built as it should have been. The portal as it stands today was part of this linear loggia, and was never conceived as a grand flourish or set piece in itself.

Hodgkinson was indeed drawn to some aspects of Futurism, in particular the idea of the sky as a transcendental plane of escape from mundane everyday life, but by his own account he was more interested in the work of the Futurist artist and sculptor Boccioni than that of Sant'Elia. Boccioni published his own Manifesto in 1914, in which he also railed against the

---

21 Antonio Sant'Elia (1914). Manifesto of Futurist Architecture, Lacerba. Reprinted in *From Futurism to Rationalism: the Origins of Modern Italian Architecture*. Architectural Design 1981.

'slavery' of architecture to the past, but emphasised the importance of emotion as a result of architectonic construction[22] –which would have struck a chord with Hodgkinson. It is hard to deny that the soaring A-frames framing the internal atria of the housing blocks give the place something of a futuristic, if not precisely Futurist, feel which even Hodgkinson does not deny: *"the A-frame is very modern – I slipped up with that! It's not traditional at all"*.[23] Actually, the A-frame structure was not central to the original design of the Brunswick, and emerged only as a by-product of changes in building legislation that meant the structure had to be engineered and executed in reinforced concrete instead of brick. Far more significant was the use of the stepped section which, for Hodgkinson, could make a direct connection with the sky while also retaining a firm link with terra firma: an ideal 'in-between place' – between the homely and the transcendent – which perfectly embodied his aspirations.

Courtyard planning and the use of brick

The essence of the Brunswick lay in the traditional notion of the organisation of an Oxbridge college – linear buildings organised internally around staircases, and externally around sheltered, bounded open spaces – an image of domestic tranquillity as in a grand medieval house or monastery.
It followed on from the work which Hodgkinson had been doing in Martin's office for Cambridge and Oxford colleges – all quiet, brick-built architecture, completely different from the rhetorical 20th-century reinforced concrete megastructure model. As Hodgkinson wrote in 1987,
> *"The collegiate plan ... breaks down the town population in appreciable stages with which we identify at different scales and levels of privacy"*.[1 (p 21)]

It is also an approach to planning that is fundamentally opposed to the suburban densities and open, dispersed layouts of the garden city movement, which, not coincidentally, had at an early stage of Le Corbusier's career been a powerful inspiration to him and directly influenced the evolution of his Ville Radieuse, with its point blocks and slab blocks surrounded by large unbounded spaces **[15]**.

Hodgkinson was antagonistic towards the suburban ideals of the garden city movement, which he felt killed the tradition of town-making by setting suburbia against urban forms. His espousal of the collegiate model accorded with Mumford's 'precinctual' approach which, predating Buchanan's *Traffic in Towns* (p 15), emphasised the social advantages it would bring in cities dominated by motor traffic. Hodgkinson saw Mumford's proposition as a straightforward enlargement and expansion of Georgian principles of town-building based on the construction of households integrated with community facilities and shops. He also cited the Palais Royale in Paris as a key antecedent, or prototype, for the Brunswick, prompting Colin Rowe's essay 'A Palais Royale for London?', in which he defined the Brunswick as a venture in 'the enclosure and definition of void'.[18 (p 28)] This represented a fundamental difference from megastructures like Moshe Safdie's Habitat at Montreal **[18]** that were concerned with "external profile, with contour, with solidity".

22 Boccioni, Umberto (1914). *Futurist painting and non-culture.*
23 PH in conversation with author Nov 2004.

But while Rowe agreed that the central space of the Brunswick was reminiscent of the typical 'attenuated Parisian courtyard' embodied in the 18th-century hotel-de-ville, he also pointed to an underlying distinction, namely the external invisibility of the Palais Royale compared to the Brunswick's almost expressionistic exterior.

> "At the Brunswick Centre the Palais Royale lingers around like an uneasy ghost. For here, the memories of classic urbanism become jostled by a range of fantasies distinctly more exotic and austere."

Rowe's analysis points to a fusion of traditional and classical urban models with a more romantic, existential dimension, in which the influence of Futurism can clearly be discerned. This casts a revealing light on the evolution of the scheme from the start.

The first scheme Hodgkinson produced was for a 'blanket' of brick courtyard buildings, internally subdivided into small vertical blocks arranged around staircases. This was subsequently modified to meet the developer's desire to minimise the cost of redeveloping the site by introducing a single large floorplate slightly elevated above street level, bordered by continuous linear blocks with relatively few points of vertical access and long horizontal internal access galleries instead: essentially the structure we see today. The blocks were higher on the internal elevation, to give a more 'civic' presence onto the precinct, and lower on the external elevation, to achieve a more domestic scale in relation to the street. The elevated plinth allowed for underground servicing and car parking, and the setback of the housing blocks from the existing street line was to accommodate the planned widening of the surrounding streets for improved traffic flow, with the removal altogether of Kenton Street and Coram Street where they traversed the newly enlarged city block.

This approach was to produce an open-ended configuration of buildings and sheltered spaces on the site, free of traffic, and capable of redefining a territory which it was felt would be better suited to the conditions of modern life. The stepped section of the blocks [19] was already in place from an early stage (preceded only briefly by the linear loggia concept), to provide 'midday sun into all the living rooms, east or west facing', and glass-enclosed 'winter-gardens' for every flat. Hodgkinson maintains that the idea of the stepped section initially came to him as a student, not from Sant'Elia and the Terrassenhäuser section, but from the less well known Elberfeld hospital project of 1928 by Marcel Breuer and Walter Gropius. But his acknowledged references are typically wide-ranging. He also points to the influence of the work of the fin-de-siècle French architect Henri Sauvage (1873-1932), one of the lesser known architects in Paris who experimented early on with newly available materials and structural technology to develop new building forms. In particular, he is noted for an apartment block design (1911) at rue Vavin in which the building steps back progressively from the street to provide each flat with a terrace [20]. Perhaps most significantly, Hodgkinson draws attention to a prototype much closer to home, the winter gardens built in the seaside town of Brighton during the 19th century, which he regarded as a far more appropriate response to the variable British climate than the open balcony.

The stepped section appealed to Hodgkinson for reasons other than the purely practical, above all because of its potential to express an existential dimension to everyday life, the fact that "it was about looking up" towards the sky. This is precisely the feature of the Brunswick flats that sociologist Richard Sennett has interpreted[24] as a severing of the connection between life inside the flats and everyday street-level activities, resulting in abstraction and alienation. For Hodgkinson, by contrast, the possibility of living 'in the clouds' was something to aspire to, allowing an escape from 'the frightful buildings [immediately] around the Brunswick' (many of which had been replaced piecemeal since the war). In other words, it appealed to his interest, born in Paris, in engaging with an existential awareness of self in the world, transcending the depressingly mundane qualities of one's immediate environs, especially in the post-war period.

Hodgkinson has described his first scheme for the Brunswick as 'a whole load of Harvey Courts', referring to the student residence he worked on with Leslie Martin for Gonville and Caius College, Cambridge, during what he has called his 'Collegiate Interlude (1957-61)'. This building [10] is arranged around an internal courtyard which is raised one storey above ground level, with the section stepped back. Banham subsequently described it as a truncated pyramid which appears "almost carved from a solid mass of brick".[25]

Harvey Court could never have been anything other than a brick building. The grid on which it was planned was 9 x 4 x 3 – which, as Hodgkinson puts it, was 'brick perfect'. Working with Leslie Martin's studio in the mid-1950s had allowed Hodgkinson to develop his commitment to brick construction that had started during his student days at the AA, and developed through his work with Alvar Aalto. As Frederic Osborn had written then[4 (p 23)], an architect's choice of materials was charged with ideological significance: *"the Ville Radieuse and the Unité d'Habitation suggested a model to be applied by good hard socialist principles in good hard modernist materials"*. The use of 'soft' brick, then, was an appropriate choice for an architect opposed to such models, and Hodgkinson's interest was fuelled not only by his love of traditional English architecture, the 'good' Arts and Crafts architects Lethaby and Voysey, but also by the work of the American Louis Kahn (1901-1974).

Kahn was not very interested in Arts and Crafts architecture, but his use of brickwork was inseparable from spatial ideas embedded in the architectures of the past. His visits to Greece, Rome and Egypt had inspired him with an interest in the monumental and spiritual qualities of ancient buildings, and he sought to recreate those qualities in a new architecture for the present. Kahn won his first major commission in 1951, an extension to the Yale Art Gallery at Yale University in New Haven, and it was his work that set Hodgkinson as a student on course in the use of brick. He suggests now that his work with Leslie Martin on the St Cross group of brick libraries in Oxford would be hailed as 'very Kahn' today, but at that time the American architect had barely established his career, and he was little known in England.

As for the Brunswick itself, it is an irony that one of its greatest claims to fame today is as a concrete building. Changes to the building regulations were responsible for the radical rethink of the construction and materials of the original scheme. Hodgkinson had grave misgivings, but recalls that other architects in the office thought that concrete really was the more appropriate

24 Sennett, Richard (1993). *The Fall of Public Man*. Faber, London.
25 Banham, Reyner (1966). *The New Brutalism: ethic or aesthetic?* Architectural Press, London.

material, because the building was *"so monumental – it was bound to look and*   *original concept*
feel more important".[26] Eventually he came round to the idea, partly because
of his concerns after Camden Council became leaseholder that the bricks
used would be of such poor quality that concrete would indeed be preferable,
and partly because he formed the view that concrete was more appropriate
for urban architecture, brick more suitable for rural buildings.

Notwithstanding the change of materials, the pervasive influence of Kahn
was indirectly highlighted by Colin Rowe in his 1971 essay, where he wrote
of the Brunswick as a modern-day Classical forum or arena. Rowe suggested
that[18] (p 28)

> *"[in] Hodgkinson's central space, it is sometimes difficult to avoid the
> impression that we are in an arena for the celebration of some archaic and
> not wholly known religious ritual. Are we in the Palace of Knossos or the Ball
> Court at Monte Alban?"*

Later, in 1989, David Hamilton Eddy, referencing Rowe, also suggested[27]
that at the Brunswick

> *"we are in a pagan world....The walkways that give access to the flats on
> the upper floors and the broad decks of the first floor bear no relation to the
> Christian cloister of Gothic and Palladian architecture...One is reminded of
> the great causeways and monuments of ancient civilisations, the Egyptian,
> the Mayan and Aztec with their ziggurats and intimations of entombment
> and human sacrifice."*

Hodgkinson concurs that "I was always interested in the ancient...
there was something there that I couldn't grapple with and nonetheless it
interested me tremendously". This interest represents another dimension of
the sense of shared ground with Kahn, and it seems likely that Kahn himself
would have appreciated Rowe's or Hamilton Eddy's romantic-classical
evocation of the Brunswick as a descendant of the ancient tradition of
monumental architecture imbued with spiritual quality.

The relationship with Coleman

Harvey Court was finished in 1962. Hodgkinson had also been working with
Martin on the adaptation of his student project for the Loughborough site in
Brixton to meet the requirements of a brief drawn up (1957) by St Pancras
Borough Council for a site in West Kentish Town. These were not exactly
courtyard projects, although the linear 'terraces', designed on a similar scale
to the existing 19th-century terraces which made up the urban fabric, were
to be grouped to form open-ended courts. The interlocking maisonettes were
comparable to those of the Unité in Marseilles, but with the significant
difference that they had a double aspect and direct access to outdoor space,
since unlike the Unité the blocks were firmly rooted in the ground, rather
than elevated above it on *pilotis*. Also banished was the Unité's 'internal
street', which, in Hodgkinson's view, was a concept with severe limitations
due to the lack of natural light and ventilation.[10] (p 25)

Developer Alec Coleman had seen the St Pancras scheme published, and
recognised its potential for resolving his problems in obtaining outline
planning consent for the Foundling site. When he approached Leslie

26 PH in conversation with author, 7.6.01.
27 Hamilton Eddy, David (1989). Castle Mythology in British Housing, *RIBA Journal* (Dec), pp 28-33.

Martin's office in 1960 the job was assigned to Hodgkinson, partly because Martin did not want to work again with Sir Edwin McAlpine, and partly because he had just been knighted and was reluctant to be involved with a speculative developer's scheme. Hodgkinson was irritated when it was later suggested that the Brunswick scheme had developed out of research conducted at the Martin Centre and published in Martin and March's 1972 publication *Urban space and structures*. The Martin Centre, which espoused a scientific, mathematical approach to architecture and planning, didn't open until 1967, and Hodgkinson claims he never had any idea that Martin and March were planning to use the Foundling site as a case study in the chapter of their book entitled *Grid as generator*. In fact, when Coleman approached the Martin studio, Hodgkinson had recently turned down Martin's offer of a partnership because he was uncomfortable with the practice's approach to design. The Brunswick project represented a great opportunity to strike out on his own, and, as he says, Coleman was a 'wonderful' client, who was willing to take risks to achieve some sort of quality.

Hodgkinson and Coleman established a good relationship from the start, largely through Coleman's surveyor, Charles Harman Hunt, who in many ways 'was the client'. Most of his work was with McAlpines, and he acted as 'a good hard pusher' for Hodgkinson and Coleman's ideas with the contractor, whom Coleman had invited in to help finance the project. McAlpines' view of the Brunswick project was crisply summarised in the words of its then chairman Sir Edwin, who stated on seeing the model: *"I think it looks like a bloody football stadium, but if you tell me it'll make money, we'll have it!"* In the end, the relationship with McAlpine seriously hampered realisation of the Brunswick, even though Hodgkinson got on well with John Derrington, head of the company's in-house engineering consultants, McAlpine Design Group. But McAlpines' early involvement was necessary to get the scheme off the ground, and Hodgkinson found that Harman Hunt, who was *"completely conservative, but very good fun [and] ... understood how much a caring architect hated people like McAlpines"*, provided an invaluable intermediary between the different parties.

Harman Hunt had an office in Mount Street, a Bentley, chauffeur, and a house on the Sussex coast. He was in his late fifties, and Hodgkinson describes him as very old-fashioned, with little knowledge or understanding of architecture, and a penchant for lunches at Simpson's in the Strand; but he had faith in the young architect, and Hodgkinson found himself well supported, and enjoyed a good working relationship with his client. When Hunt announced in 1965 that the job was dead, because McAlpines had mismanaged its investments and run out of money, he agreed with Hodgkinson's suggestion that they approach Camden Council, and it was Hunt who hammered out the deal with them. Ultimately, he couldn't save either Hodgkinson or Coleman from McAlpine's heavy-handed cuts and antagonism. By the time Coleman was ousted and Hodgkinson forced to resign in 1970, Hodgkinson had had enough of the project: he had been unable to do anything like the design work he'd wanted to or develop his architectural ideas during his period on the Brunswick, because he had spent nearly all his time on the telephone dealing with administrative matters.

The Outline Planning scheme (1960-1963)

Hodgkinson's first idea for a grid of eight blocks, with vertical access staircases, bedrooms looking onto internal courtyards, and living rooms looking onto public space [21], was quickly replaced at the developer's wishes by a layout of two parallel linear blocks, with fewer staircases and long access galleries. Initially these were solid blocks, with double-aspect flats running from front to back; the space between the two blocks was a relatively narrow street rather than a precinct or piazza. This evolved into an arcade, with a circular recital hall placed centrally at the intersection of north-south/east-west axes [22]. Fifty-four shops on each side were proposed, with a department store on two floors. There was also a petrol station facing onto Marchmont Street, and extensive car parking, along with two electricity substations, under the elevated floor plate in a double basement.

The central axis through the scheme is clearly shown in the early drawings to be aligned with the east side of Queen Square to the south, and it is intriguing to note the superficial similarities between the Brunswick concept and the Charles Holden schemes for the University of London in the early 1930s. These were to provide new university accommodation in a long 'spine' stretching from Montague Place in the south to Byng Place in the north, presenting a monumental, formal façade of advancing and retreating bays to Malet Street with a series of entrance courtyards . In the third scheme for the university the central, raised spine was located at the centre of a linear double grid of internal and open courtyards stretching along the site [8].

Although comparisons can be made between this project and Hodgkinson's work, and he acknowledges that he briefly saw it in Martin's office prior to the Brunswick commission, he says he was much more strongly influenced by an unexecuted 18th-century plan for the Foundling Estate, by a forgotten architect named Merryweather. This proposal comprised a long wide street stretching from Queen Square to Tavistock Place, and, as Hodgkinson later put it – 'if they can do it, we can!' He had a clear vision of the new development as *"a major public place on a proposed pedestrian route linking the rail termini of Euston Road with the offices of Holborn".*[1 (p 21)]

Whatever the possible precedents, it is clear that the concept of a monumental axial scheme had been in the air for a long time, and that the Brunswick proposal was not as radical as one might think. In any case, it was a vastly preferable option to the alternative of high-rise tower blocks and slabs. By the early 1960s traffic considerations had also become paramount, road widening seemed to be inevitable, and everyone assumed that the shops on Marchmont Street would disappear. The long Brunswick shopping arcade was regarded as an appropriate and well-conceived replacement for, not a duplication of, Marchmont Street, which would be taken over by fast-flowing traffic, and the planners therefore stipulated that a new shopping frontage should be inward-facing, and the street-line of the new housing set back behind that of the original buildings on the site.

Because the profitable hotel and large office uses had been separated out and allocated to Site B, Site A became a relatively 'pure' housing scheme, still mixed-use, but only with uses directly complementary to the main programme. Apart from the shops, a small number of 'professional chambers', mainly to replace doctors' surgeries already in the area, were included over the shops [9]. The shops opened onto a wide terrace which was conceived as a public square or pleasure garden looking down into the piazza below, and connected to it by a grand staircase.

The speculative scheme of 1964: A-frame and wintergardens

On winning Outline Planning consent in 1963, the developer decided the scheme should be modified to meet a more typical speculative brief, which Hodgkinson worked on for a further year. The first major alteration was the replacement of the circular recital hall by a covered shopping hall as the focus of the arcade. Hodgkinson wrote

> *"It will give a meeting place to the area and allow the terrace above to become one large space: a piece of quiet tree-lined ground (not just a raised deck) separating the housing from street bustle".* [10] (p 25)

The housing allocation was also altered, the number of 'high-grade' units being reduced to achieve a better commercial mix; the solid housing blocks were also redesigned, with the introduction of a concrete A-frame carrying a tier of single-aspect housing on each side, one facing outwards (the 'perimeter' block), and one inwards (the taller, 'main' block) [19].

This was a dramatic structural innovation to the scheme, a significant departure from the quiet, load-bearing brick approach which Hodgkinson first favoured. It is not surprising, given his happy working relationship with the engineer Felix Samuely during his student years, that he turned to Samuely for advice on this development of the project. Once the decision had been made to proceed with the A-frame, Hodgkinson was keen to show it off, and maximise the potential of the internal space both to function as an internal street and also as an expressive device which, in the words of Boccioni, works as an *"internal (architectonic) construction [which] gives rise to emotion".* [23] On the other hand, he wanted to stick to a largely invisible, inexpressive, load-bearing brick structure for the volume of the blocks, combined with brick facing and concrete render. This relaxed, eclectic attitude to construction and the ideology of materials free of dogmatism was at odds with the attitude of some of his neo-Corbusian contemporaries – and a good thing too, in view of McAlpines' limitations. McAlpines had built the Dorchester hotel in the 1930s, but had no interest in ordinary housing, nor any in promoting innovation in structural solutions or construction methods. According to Hodgkinson, they didn't even believe in pre-casting concrete, although in the end they did pre-cast the housing floor slabs, so that for the duration of the project there was an enormous crowd of navvies on site, in scenes that looked positively Victorian. It looked very weird to architects brought up with the innovative pre-fabricated structural approaches propounded by Buckminster Fuller.

With the introduction of the A-frame, the open terraces in the outline scheme were now enclosed as glazed wintergardens. The second glass screen to the rooms behind would have allowed them to be used either as extensions to the living space or as open balconies. The asymmetrically paired, linear tiers of raked glazing, glinting in the light [3], were subsequently to become the defining feature of the Brunswick as an urban landmark, even after Ministry of Housing regulations forced a change in the design in the next phase of revisions.

The Council scheme (1965-1970)

In 1965 Hodgkinson embarked on further modifications to the scheme, in the hope of making it attractive to the council. The key factor in this Council Scheme was the further reduction of the housing mix and the size of the flats, but other changes were also necessary. The Ministry of Housing had specified that flats must have an open balcony, and would not accept the wintergardens as such, so the glazing component was cut back to leave half the space per flat as open balcony, and half as the single-glazed 'greenhouse' that we see today. The developer wanted to see the shop units increased in size, and a large basement supermarket added, although this was later rejected. The recital hall, meanwhile, after much debate, became a cinema (the ABC Bloomsbury, from 1986 the Renoir) in the basement, located underneath the Brunswick Square portico. Despite the general reduction of the scheme, Hodgkinson managed to persuade John Derrington, McAlpines' engineer, to retain the design of foundations and structure appropriate for the addition of a further storey on top of the building at some future date, and planning permission for that potential top floor was obtained the same year.

Once the council had bought the lease of the housing component and appointed its own architect, Bikerdike Allen and Rich, to supervise the work, Hodgkinson's involvement became more precarious. He was happy to liase with Camden's Chief Architect, S A G Cook (who oversaw a number of innovative housing schemes showing the influence of the Brunswick elsewhere in the Borough), and enjoyed a good relationship not only with Bill Allen, whose job it was to approve the technical aspects of the working drawings for Camden, but also with John Derrington, who looked after the whole construction programme, including structural and services engineering, for McAlpines. Even so, Hodgkinson found it increasingly difficult to accept the developers' lower standards, and also what he describes as 'misbehaviour' on both McAlpines' and Camden's sides in blatantly breaching the terms of the planning consent in various ways. In 1970 (three days before his 40th birthday), when he had completed all the drawings and obtained the necessary consents, McAlpines told him his services were no longer required, and his outstanding fees would be settled only if he resigned.

The project grinds to a halt (1972)

Hodgkinson was subsequently replaced by L Brian Ingram, architect to the contractors, who applied for permission to omit six staircases connecting level A (precinct level) to level C (the terrace), which was approved, and also to omit the connecting pedestrian slab between the two sides of the terrace, which was rejected – although the link that was eventually built was a very rough and ready version of what had been intended. In 1972, Ingram was replaced by T P Bennett and Son.

It was the latter who made the decision to scrap the glazed roof of the shopping hall, which was to have been *"London's first glass-covered shopping galleria since the arcades of Piccadilly had been built"*.[9] [(p 25)] Also jettisoned was the cream-coloured paint finish to the fairface concrete façades intended by Hodgkinson, along with the tiling, paintwork and decorative brick slip-work he had specified for the shopping area:

"painted stucco and concrete (Crown Commissioners' cream, as for Regent's

Park) for the housing, with bright painted colour, bricks, tiles and mosaic as foreground in the shopping street with its covered galleria, fountains and richly patterned pavements". [9] (p 25)

Towards the end of 1972 building work came to a stop: "*a desultory halt at Handel Street..., the Council having completely reneged on its own planning consent, not because of rising costs* [the oil crisis was yet to come] *but to reduce the value of the development*", wrote Hodgkinson later.

Building work was not resumed until Spring 2005, despite a series of planning applications for redevelopment made between 1992 and 2000, during which period the Brunswick was recommended for Listing and finally designated a Grade II building of architectural and historic significance. In Hodgkinson's words "*it was a bungled, funny contract, yet it's still considered an interesting building by some people*". Despite a highly convoluted procurement process and repeated renegotiations of the planning consents, it remains a building of quality and considerable impact, iconic in its forward thinking, which made a radical break with zoning regulations and, moreover, gave back 70% of the land area as public or private open space, 40% more than the old estate.

The Brunswick as vehicle of domestic life

In 1963, with the design of the Brunswick proceeding apace, the Daily Mail Ideal Home Exhibition celebrated its 40th anniversary, entitled 'Design 1963'. That title alone was an indication of how far the idea of modern design had captured the popular imagination. The previous year, the exhibition had featured An Adventure in Design, by Trevor Smith, and The McLean Split Level House, both conceived as self-consciously modern homes, amongst the 'village' of show houses in a variety of styles forming the centrepiece of each exhibition. Seven years earlier, in 1956 (the year before Patrick Hodgkinson started work at Leslie Martin's office), the Exhibition had celebrated its jubilee year by reinstating a so-called House of the Future alongside the village, reviving a short-lived tradition started in 1928. This house, designed by the 'new Brutalist' architects Alison and Peter Smithson, was a plastic structure intended to be wholly mass-produced as a unit, with various automated functions (including functions we take for granted today, such as remote controls for TV and lighting, and a doorbell answerphone) and a self-cleaning capacity. In the same year, the *This is Tomorrow* exhibition, co-organised by the Smithsons at the Whitechapel Art Gallery, had created a stir amongst artistic and intellectual circles. Exhibits such as Richard Hamilton's collage 'Just what is it that makes today's homes so different, so appealing?' focused attention on the home as an arena for radical thought.

Between the mid-1950s and mid-1960s, then, there was considerable interest in rethinking traditional models of the home, both at an intellectual and a more populist level. The notion of modernity had permeated the thinking of the general public, and ordinary people were prepared to contemplate fairly forward-looking ideas about the organisation and setting of their domestic lives.

When Tate Britain staged its retrospective of 1960s art and architecture in 2004, under the title *This Was Tomorrow*, it made deliberate play on the theme of the Whitechapel exhibition almost 50 years before. The Tate event included the Brunswick and other landmark buildings of the period, alongside Pop-art canvases, erotic sculptures, robotic installations, and material from the *Destruction in Art* symposium, highlighting the subversive and avant-garde aspects of the cultural context. Whereas the Brunswick may be fêted as an example of modern design, ahead of its time, Patrick Hodgkinson saw himself essentially as a traditionalist in domestic design, and experiments such as the Smithsons' House of the Future were of little interest to him. He deliberately designed the Brunswick flats not to be ultra-modern, but homely.

He was, he says, 'a bit dreary' about domestic ideas, not influenced at all by futuristic notions of home life. *"For myself, the concept of family life with children was entirely traditional"*, he writes[11 (p 26)], and this was reflected in the design of the dwelling units at the Brunswick. Hodgkinson greatly admired the 'magical' 14th- and 15th-century great houses of England, with an interplay between open and closed, public and private, grand and intimate spaces, which reflected domestic ritual and 'gave an ordered hierarchy to life' (see p 24). In the first Brunswick scheme, Hodgkinson drew on this model to achieve an open, airy T-shaped living space, juxtaposed with a band of closed service rooms intended to shield the habitable rooms from street noise [23]. The wintergarden concept, drawing on 19th-century precedent, allowed the main living space to be opened up completely to the external space, in a manner that also reflected the Modernist use of a glazed envelope to blur the boundaries between interior and exterior.

In the earlier Brixton and St Pancras housing schemes, Hodgkinson had reworked the Unité idea of split-level flats with double-height, glass-fronted living spaces overlooking the park, and services shunted to the back of the unit, abutting the internal street. Hodgkinson designed the kitchen as the largest living space, one-and-a-half storeys high, opening onto a terrace, with a smaller 'best room', or parlour, located off it, a half-level up, and the main bedroom with its own shower unit located beyond that. Children's bedrooms and bathroom were located half a level below the kitchen, at entrance level.

> *"Family banter would take place in a light, airy 'open' space, but old and young could withdraw to the privacy of their own 'closed' realms, the young being near the front door for their friends."* [1 (p 21)]

By contrast, the LCC's scheme for the Brixton site meant that *"family life had to be sustained in a laboratory kitchen not large enough for a decent table, because the living-room was kept for Sunday best"*.

The Brunswick project *"was about a different lifestyle than the project for St Pancras."* The kitchen was integrated within a large living space, off which the bedrooms opened, on both sides in two- and three-bedroom units, on one side only in one-bedroom units. The kitchen zone had a window overlooking the access gallery (and beyond, at the upper, open levels), but otherwise commanded an open view across the living-room and out through the glazed winter garden. The living space could be opened up to the wintergarden, which formed a glazed band across the whole frontage of the flat, although that would then impinge on the privacy of the bedrooms, which also had external doors opening into the wintergarden area.

The introduction of Parker Morris Housing Standards in 1964 has often been cited to explain the larger area of council housing units of that period than in more recent models, but in fact, when the Brunswick was transferred to Camden council the scale had to be reduced, and the wintergarden had to be replaced by open balconies; this resulted in balconies set above floor level, poorly drained and prone to leaks, and living-room fenestration set uncomfortably high in the wall. The wintergarden had been conceived as a clever response to the climate, which frequently renders open balconies unusable – even for hanging out washing, which was of course swiftly banned at the Brunswick. Residents were also told to hang net curtains across their picture windows, another requirement that would have been obviated by the double glazed screen of the winter garden design.

As for the internal layout, the scheme as built saw a curiously proportioned shoulder-height partition installed between kitchen and living-space, in place of the waist-high counter and strip of overhead storage, while the bedrooms were grouped to one side of the living-room, accessed separately and individually off an enlarged entrance hall. En-suite washing facilities, and separate WC, were also jettisoned in favour of a single combined bathroom and toilet, also opening off the entrance hall. These changes led to a general loss of habitable space in favour of increased circulation space and self-containment of bedrooms [24]: in other words, a reversion to a more cellular, 19th-century model, as opposed to the spatial interplay of the medieval prototypes which Hodgkinson so enjoyed.

Thus, Hodgkinson's 'traditionalism' in domestic design, coupled with a questioning approach to the model established by the Unité in Marseilles, had led him to a more flexible and innovative approach to the internal organisation of dwellings for the post-war era than the authorities seemed willing to consider. When it came to the secondary fittings of the units, he did evoke an explicitly modern, indeed futuristic, model – that of the Dymaxion House, designed in 1929 by Richard Buckminster Fuller, the American inventor who saw, and to an extent realised, the potential of new lightweight, industrially-produced materials to create the homes of the future [25].

The Dymaxion House was made of lightweight steel, duraluminium and plastic, and was suspended from a central mast from which the rooms radiated on a hexagonal plan. The principles were applied some years later to produce temporary shelters, but were never fully embraced by the construction industry. The house pointed the way to a prefabricated approach to the production of homes for both the external envelope and the internal fittings, which was a direct inspiration to architects working at that time. Hodgkinson always assumed that the secondary fittings of the Brunswick would be prefabricated along the same lines, but in fact the 'incredibly simple-minded' approach of the contractor – reluctant even to pre-cast the concrete elements – made it extremely unlikely from the start that such a route to the completion of the units would ever be taken.

3 Critical reception & the saga of redevelopment plans

Illustrations numbered in square brackets are shown on pp 88 ff.

In 1975, two years after building had ceased, the London Borough of Camden was sufficiently proud of its achievements at the Brunswick to publish a pamphlet publicising the building. It stated, in evocative terms, *The Brunswick Centre was conceived not as a city in itself but to provide a nucleus for future housing development in the neighbourhood. As architecture it makes a statement of permanence; its outer shell will present the same face to many generations, but inside it can adapt itself to different kinds of life and activity that successive inhabitants may bring.*

This description revealed a clear awareness of the significance of the Brunswick as architecture as well as the Council's commitment to new housing provision for the community. The project significantly influenced housing design by the borough architects' department in the decade that followed: schemes such as Maiden Lane by Benson and Forsyth, and, most distinctively, Alexandra Road, NW8 [26] by Neave Brown (1972-8) – although Hodgkinson himself was always critical of Brown for being '100% Le Corbusier' in his outlook.[1]

Reference to the building's potential adaptability was reiterated in 2000 by DOCOMOMO in response to English Heritage's recommendation for Listing.[2] It made a case for the Brunswick as the embodiment of

"*a framework that accepts and assumes change within it over time.... The great space-making structure which accommodates the communal spaces and the fundamental relationships of parts is fixed, and the detailed pattern of uses and components within it reflects change.*"

DOCOMOMO opposed EH's recommendation for Listing, because the new freeholder, Allied Properties plc, had come up with a plan to refurbish the building, and DOCOMOMO argued that Listing would impede its successful realisation. The Department of Culture, Media and Sport nevertheless proceeded with the Grade II Listing of the Brunswick that same year[3], pointing out that Listing did not preclude change.

The Brunswick as megastructure

Hodgkinson himself always disliked the definition of the Brunswick as a megastructure as he considered the social concept of the *village* far more apt. He felt there was only one critic who grasped the essence of the Brunswick,

1 PH in conversation with the author, Nov 2004.
2 Cooke, Catherine (2000): letter from Chair, DOCOMOMO-UK (UK branch, International Working Party for Documentation and Conservation of Buildings, Sites and Neighbourhoods of the Modern Movement), to Kenneth Humphreys, Buildings, Monuments and Sites Division of the UK Government Department of Culture, Media and Sport, 15 Mar.
3 DCMS Schedule (2000) 798-1/95/10155, Brunswick Square (West side), 1-187a O'Donnell Court, 1-212a Foundling Court, Renoir Cinema, shops (The Brunswick Shopping Centre), basement car-park, and attached ramps, steps and studios. 25th Amendment of the 53rd List of Buildings of Special Architectural or Historic Interest, London Borough of Camden.

namely David Hamilton Eddy, in a piece written for the *RIBA Journal* much later (1989). Hamilton Eddy described the building in architectural-anthropological terms as a composition of

> *"two related but ultimately separate dimensions, each of which is facing in opposite directions, both practically and symbolically....These can be seen as traditional-communal and futurist-autonomous."*

He defined the former as the public area, the *"thriving bazaar of shops... open to the surrounding neighbourhood"*, and the latter as the housing:

> *"a different world...rows of glazed apartments...like the serried ranks of two alien armies...a dream world, familiar and entrancing and disturbing at once...."* [4]

Hamilton Eddy celebrated what he saw as the Futurist spirit of the housing design, a liberating force within the 'conventional restraining order of Georgian and Victorian London, with its closely arranged social system where everyone is 'placed' and knows their place.' He understood the idealism of the architect's social ambitions, and the source of his inspiration as a heady fusion of traditional forms with a very modern notion of social identity and individuality in a world that had been turned upside down by two world wars.

Perhaps it was easier for Eddy to understand the Brunswick in looking back across a period of 15 years, during which the strict ideologies of architectural practice had fragmented into a kaleidoscopic pluralism under the impact of important texts such as Robert Venturi's *Complexity and contradiction in architecture*,[5] and the ensuing evolution of post-Modernism. But in the period immediately before and after completion of work on the site, architecture critics were determinedly pursuing an appropriate label for the project that would locate it unambiguously within Modernist architectural history. Inevitably, *megastructure* was the one most readily seized on.

Banham's book on the subject[6] was not published until 1976; the megastructure epithet had already been evoked in 1972, when the *Architectural Review* published a critique by Theo Crosby in its special issue celebrating the conclusion of works at the Brunswick. Crosby's appraisal[7] was positive in some aspects, but highly critical in others. He saw the Brunswick as an example of the negative impact of industrialisation on choice and variety in the city, where

> *"tidiness and simple-mindedness have taken over, and...the possibilities for change and growth are permanently inhibited...by the solidity of the architecture and the nature of the construction."*

Above all, he said,

> *"the problem lies in the urban concept. The Brunswick Centre is perhaps the first built example of the idea of the urban megastructure – a building that is a city, rather than being merely a component in a city....The megastructure, because it is self-contained, does not integrate with its surroundings. It is an alien growth, and for its own success it must eat up the surroundings as quickly as possible so as to impose its own order and system on every aspect of life there."* [7]

To a large extent, Crosby laid the blame for this state of affairs on the developers –

4 Hamilton Eddy, D. 'Castle Mythology in British Housing', *RIBA Journal* Dec 1989, p 28.
5 Venturi, Robert (1966/1977). *Complexity and contradiction in architecture*. Museum of Modern Art, New York; Architectural Press, London.
6 Banham, Reyner (1976). *Megastructure: Urban futures of the recent past*. Thames & Hudson, London.
7 Crosby, Theo (1972). *Architectural Review* Oct, pp 211-212.

"all big schemes are only viable through economies of scale, which allow the
profits to come back to relatively few promoters....Any protest on loss of visual
or social amenity is easily ignored in pursuit of an economic goal."

He was generous enough to say that
"the Brunswick Centre proves that a good architect will somehow, in spite of
endless disappointment and compromise, manage to produce a meaningful
piece of architecture."

But his condemnation of the megastructure concept embodied, as he saw it,
by the Brunswick, was fairly direct.

By contrast, Banham's appraisal, which cited Crosby, was more positive.
Banham stated unequivocally that the project was *"saved by...composition and*
design from the kind of cheerless chaos that infected so much of the less determined
'megastructure' housing of that period."

Banham had a natural enthusiasm for megastructures, witness his
comprehensive survey of the type. By his account, the Brunswick was pretty
much the shining star of megastructure design in Britain. Starting with
its origins in Sant'Elia's *The Futurist city* (1914), and Le Corbusier's Fort
l'Empereur project (1931) [27], Banham proceeded to survey a wide range of
megastructure schemes from Britain, Europe, America, Canada and Japan,
firmly placing the Brunswick in the framework of a global phenomenon. In
1964 the Japanese architect Fumihiko Maki described a megastructure as
"a large frame in which all the functions of a city or part of a city are housed.
It has been made possible by present-day technology." [8]

By then, various experiments in realising the concept had been
undertaken or initiated. Banham notes, among others, Basil Spence's Sea
and Ships Pavilion at the Festival of Britain (1951), schemes for Sheffield
University by the Smithsons and Stirling (1953), and Camino's project for
a new university in Tucuman, Mexico (1952). Banham attributes these
developments partly to a tide of interest in vernacular architectures and
natural habitats, which between 1964 and 1965 found a focus in Bernard
Rudofsky's highly influential exhibition 'Architecture without architects' at
the Museum of Modern Art in New York. He also makes a link to a parallel
revival of interest in Expressionism and Futurism, as a romanticised vision
of modern technology, which Hodgkinson certainly to some extent shared.

Le Corbusier was subsequently to develop the Fort l'Empereur idea
in the form of the Unité d'Habitation [12], realised on five sites in France
during the 1950s and 1960s. However, many of the later projects that
Banham identified as 'megastructural', such as Archigram's City Interchange
(1963) or Plug-In City (1964) [28], Moshe Safdie's Habitat (1967) in
Montreal [18], Stanley Tigerman's Instant City project (1968), Buckminster
Fuller and Shoji Sadao's Triton City project (1968) or Paul Rudolph's Lower
Manhattan Expressway project (1970) [29] were much more extrovert and
explicitly innovative in structural and technological terms, and manifested a
very different architectural spirit from Hodgkinson's: as he puts it, succinctly,
"Oh, Archigram, never." [9]

By contrast, there is much more common ground between the Brunswick
and other significant built examples of megastructures in Britain. These

8 Maki, Fumihiko (1964). *Investigations in collective form.* Special Publication No. 2. Washington
University School of Architecture, St Louis, MO.
9 PH letter to the author, 22.5.01.

include L. Hugh Wilson and Geoffrey Copcut's Cumbernauld Town Centre (1960) [30], A D Cooke and Partners' Anglia Town Square, Norwich (1966), Roger Harrison (New Town Corporation)'s Runcorn Shopping Centre (1967) [31] Neave Brown's Alexandra Road, (1968) [26], and Ralph Erskine's Byker Wall, Newcastle (1968) [32]. However, most of these schemes were designed for New Towns or institutional use, while Brown and Erskine's local authority housing schemes do not accommodate a mixed-use programme like the Brunswick. The much earlier Barbican Centre, London [33] (designed 1956, though not completed until much later) is also sometimes considered as an example of the megastructure, but the style and conception are very different, comprising high-rise towers, brick surface treatments, and a lack of everyday shopping amenities.

According to Hodgkinson, Lasdun admitted privately that his design for the Institute of Education had been 'cribbed' from the Brunswick, barely two blocks to the west, although the rectilinear glass and concrete form of the Lasdun building gives it a very different appearance, except possibly from the back [34]. Lasdun was also a great admirer of Harvey Court, which had influenced his earlier University of East Anglia student housing scheme [35], described by Banham as a series of 'concrete ziggurats'. Of Erskine's project, which is visually very different – a long, flat, high brick wall on one side, breaking out into an anarchic jumble of balconies and verandas on the other [32] – Hodgkinson later said "I never accepted Byker until I went there in the late 1970s and had almost never before seen such happy faces on a council estate, except perhaps at Taylor & Green's village additions for Loddon District Council."[10] Hodgkinson considered the Alexandra Road scheme by Neave Brown [26] as the sole example of the megastructural idea expressed at the Brunswick that was realised elsewhere. However, he regarded it as a much more Corbusian, formalistic project, which placed great emphasis on pure structural integrity and could not accommodate the 'messy' mix of uses in the Brunswick programme. Brown suggested in his critique of the Brunswick that the lack of a pure skeleton structure (as opposed to load-bearing brick walls) and of free, adaptable space was disappointing, and that a mixed-use programme could never be successfully achieved by speculative developers:

> *"The vast complex of ingredients that must be recognised and included in responsible city development is beyond the imagination and resources of speculative developers, no matter how responsible they may be."* [11]

Neither architect seemed able to appreciate fully the work of the other.

In 1974, a development near Marble Arch in London, now called St George's Fields [36], was built by architects Design 5 for the Utopian Voluntary Housing Group. It bears a striking resemblance to the Brunswick, but on a much smaller, tamer, more domestic scale. Banham described it as

> *"a cluster of mini-megastructures of entirely routine construction – Terrassenhäuser A-frames, semi-underground parking, pedestrian bridges – mini-megastructures as an acceptable format for upper-middle-class housing".* [12]

10 See note 9. Taylor & Green was a Suffolk-based practice, specialising in rural housing, which Hodgkinson attempted to buy in the mid-1970s when the partners sold up.
11 Brown, Neave (1972). Brunswick Centre and Central Urban Redevelopment. *Architectural Review* Vol 152 (Oct), p 212.
12 Note 6, p 189.

The brief heyday of the megastructure as the visionary architectural vehicle of social idealism seemed to be over. As Hodgkinson points out, post-Modernism was dawning, and architects were facing a different climate of opinion both aesthetically and in what was deemed acceptable in the clearance and replacement of the urban fabric. In 1968, the megastructure form had already been condemned by planner Peter Hall in an article entitled 'Monumental Follies'[13], which lambasted the clearance mentality of the authorities. In his book *Cities of tomorrow* he recalls the impact of the redevelopment proposals for Covent Garden Market in London, and the tide of protest which they provoked, culminating in what he calls a national nervous breakdown in 1968: *"the whole of Great Britain was at that time involved in saving something"*. In 1971, Rod Hackney, future champion of so-called 'community architecture' and President of the RIBA, organised a high-profile campaign to save traditional housing in Macclesfield from clearance. In 1973 the first General Improvement Area programme was completed by architect Nigel Melhuish, as a viable alternative to slum clearance and redevelopment at the Flower Streets in Liverpool, an estate of substandard 19th-century dockworkers' cottages that he regenerated.[14] It did not take long for the concept of the megastructure to become discredited, and the publication of Banham's book[6] (p 42) in 1976 was in many ways a valediction.

'Brutalist' Brunswick

"It's always been known as a Brutalist building but I had no intention of it ending up that way." Patrick Hodgkinson, 1998[15]

"Like other survivors of Britain's most bloody-minded architectural movement, the brutalists of the 1960s, he [Hodgkinson] is sticking to his guns." Deyan Sudjic, 2000[16]

The Brutalist strand of British architectural history evolved in the 1950s within the architects' offices of the LCC as a reaction against the so-called 'Welfare State' ideology of an older generation of architects. This was also known, in derogatory terms, as the 'William Morris Revival', or 'People's Detailing' – exemplified by the Festival of Britain architecture, which Hodgkinson had so enjoyed, but which many young architects derided as anodyne and populist. Its primary sources were the 19th-century English Arts and Crafts tradition, and the State-sponsored architecture of Sweden, both of which were characterised by the use of brick, and had a special place in Hodgkinson's heart.

The 'Brutalists', by contrast, called for an 'anti-design' approach in which the use of 'raw' and 'exposed' materials, devoid of finishes and claddings, was fundamental. Husband-and-wife architects Peter and Alison Smithson were central to the movement, developing what has been called an 'anthropological aesthetic', strongly coloured by the influence

13 Hall, Peter (1968). 'Monumental Follies' *New Society* Vol 12 No. 317 (24 Oct).
14 Melhuish, Nigel (2001). *The Flower Streets, Kirkdale, Liverpool 1870-2001: A Brief History*. Design and production by Francis Cawley. London.
15 Tomlin, Julie (1998). 'Brunswick Centre architect admits block is an eyesore' *Camden New Journal* 15 Jan.
16 Sudjic, Deyan (2000). Whose building is it anyway? *Observer Review* 19 Mar.

of iconographic Modern Movement buildings – notably the Marseilles Unité, Mies van der Rohe's Silk Factory at Krefeld (1932-3) and Lafayette Park, Detroit (1959 onwards) – as well as the vernacular architectures and settlements of Japan and Europe. They later wrote, as spokesmen for the movement,

> "What is new about the New Brutalism among Movements is that it finds its closest affinities not in a past architectural style, but in peasant dwelling forms, which have style and are stylish but were never modish: a poetry without rhetoric. We see architecture as a direct statement of a way of life and, in the past, ordinary prosaic life has been most succinctly, economically, tersely expressed in the peasant farms and the impedimenta of Mediterranean rural life that Le Corbusier has made respectable." [17]

They embraced the techniques of industrialised mass production as the authentic expression of a modern vernacular, in particular the use of concrete, resulting in an aesthetic which was invested with profound ethical and ideological significance, and which, in its ruggedness and roughness, was antithetical to the smooth, bland aesthetic of 'People's Detailing'.

By 1966, the new Brutalism was sufficiently well-established for Reyner Banham to produce a book charting the movement, in which he incorporated a sub-category, the 'Brick Brutalists', to embrace those architects working in brick as opposed to concrete, who he felt still qualified as Brutalist on account of the exposed way in which the material was used, without traditional finishes. Banham included Hodgkinson's Harvey Court in this section, which he described as appearing 'almost carved from a solid mass of brick', and he also suggested that the planning concept was related to the Smithsons' interest in ancient sites: it had, he said, 'the air of a sacred enclosure'.[18]

Hodgkinson, however, had deliberately avoided being taught by Peter Smithson in his last year at the Architectural Association, because he fundamentally disagreed with his approach. He said that the acclaimed school building at Hunstanton [37]

> "appeared to me to be the very opposite of what a school should be and something like Team X [set up by the Smithsons and others as an alternative to Le Corbusier's Congrès International d'Architecture Moderne], which was political, was the last way I wanted to make my architecture."

He consciously distanced himself from Brutalism, stating

> "I myself reject Brutalism (which actually came from Sweden) because I felt it was inhuman and just a fashionable gimmick." [19]

However, Smithson admired the Brunswick, and had chosen to include the Brunswick in the Brutalist canon.

The Brunswick's unfinished concrete surfaces drew Theo Crosby's attention in his article[7] for the *Architectural Review* cited on p 42.

> "This defiance of new concrete set in one of the most consistent brick environments in London is what makes the project interesting as an urban adventure, and worthy of analysis."

Crosby took the Brunswick's use of exposed, fairface concrete without any surface finishes to be charged with ideological significance – whereas

17 Smithson, Alison and Peter (1973). *Without rhetoric – an architectural aesthetic 1955-72.* Latimer New Dimensions, London.
18 Banham, R (1966). *The New Brutalism: ethic or aesthetic?* Architectural Press, London
19 PH letter to the author, 22.5.01.

it was the vicissitudes of procurement and the incomplete process of
construction that had led to the building's final appearance. Far from being
a statement of purist aesthetic and ideological conviction, the Brunswick
embodied the ambiguities, conflicts, and compromises that determine the
outcome of most real-life large architecture projects.

vicissitudes

Reactions of the general press

While the architecture critics set out to find a label for the Brunswick,
journalists and writers from other disciplines felt compelled to voice their
reactions on seeing the dramatic profile of the building emerge from the
wasteland of demolished Georgian houses. In the trade press there had
been a fairly muted response to Hodgkinson's resignation in 1970, which
nevertheless raised concerns about the quality of the finished building[20].
The following year, Peter Murray wrote an article[21] for *Architectural Design* in
which he suggested that the

> *"contorted history [of the project] gives rise to doubts about the viability of this
> sort of co-operation between developer and local council...It will be a tragedy
> for the development if it is not completed....If it should be blocked at one end
> by the TA [see p 19] it is likely to become an environmental desert."*

Not only that, but

> *"Council tenants, unlike the middle-income, middle-class inhabitants initially
> expected on the site, are unlikely to be respecters of the clean contemporary
> lines of the exterior",*

though what he meant by that, apart from the possibility of washing being
hung out to dry on the balconies, is not clear. Nonetheless, he concluded
that the Brunswick was

> *"a building of class – a stylish building...[and] a pleasant architectural space
> that makes a fitting successor to the graceful square and streets that once
> adorned the area."*

Other commentators were not so positive. In *Private Eye* in 1970, the poet
John Betjeman slammed the development in scathing and sarcastic terms,
in a piece suggestively entitled the "New Barbarism':[22]

> *"Tentative attempts were made [at barbarism] in Bloomsbury, always a home
> of revolution, with [Charles Holden's] London University Senate House
> building (1932); and all progressive people must be grateful to this University
> for destroying so many of the Georgian squares and terraces so long a
> notorious impediment to enlightened planning. I am unable to find the names
> of the designers of the brilliant complex which our photograph shows...The
> stepped fenestration above is awaiting not tomatoes, but human fecundity...
> The bold structural concrete bones from which the...conservatories are slung
> convey at once a sense of compactness and regimented irregularity".*

Betjeman was not alone in his conservative views. Stephen Gardiner,
in the *Observer Review* the same year, described a 'conflict of scales'
accounting for 'the peculiar air of placelessness', a 'seemingly endless

---

20 'Architect and Developer part company'. News, 8 Apr 1970, *Architects' Journal*, p 842.
Architectural Press, London.
21 Murray, Peter (1971). 'Foundling Estate, Bloomsbury' *Architectural Design* Oct, p 605. Academy
Editions, London.
22 Betjeman, John (1971). 'The New Barbarism', Nooks and Corners, *Private Eye* 13.8.71.

perspective view', and 'an appalling feeling of vertigo'.[23] Not until the following year (1971) did a more complimentary piece[24] appear in the *Daily Telegraph*, written by one Violet Johnstone, in which she said the Brunswick was 'reminiscent of Mediterranean shores' – an evocative figure of speech which she then rather undermined by suggesting that it might equally be seen as a laboratory building, 'with all that glass', or a hospital. Johnstone was otherwise enthusiastic in her appraisal, describing it as 'Bloomsbury's answer to the Barbican', commending the 'imaginative air of the exterior', and demonstrating an appreciation of the intent to 'recreate the Bloomsbury of a century ago' as a vibrant, mixed urban quarter. She also reported that the first tenants, who had taken up residence in the autumn of the previous year, 'find it provides a sense of identity'.

In December 1973, the *Observer Magazine* ran a more favourable piece than Gardiner's. Another female author, Ena Kendall, wrote[25] of the glazed terraces, again in somewhat exotic terms, as

"*a series of backward-stepping, glass-fronted tiers, suggesting a ziggurat, the pyramid-type Babylonian temple.*"

She also dismissed the term 'urban megastructure' as a 'lumpish description', and quoted some of the tenants' views which showed an appreciation of the new environment, certainly compared with other council estates.

By this time, the *Architectural Review* had also published its special issue (October 1972) on the Brunswick (containing Theo Crosby's and Neave Brown's analyses[7,11]). A large number of overseas architecture magazines, from France, Japan, Germany, the Netherlands, Switzerland, Denmark, Italy and the USA, had also picked up on the Brunswick and published reports, though these were mostly fairly factual accounts with standard images and plans. In the meantime, the home press had quietened down, its interest not to be reawakened until 1990, when the first planning application for the redevelopment of the Brunswick created a furore and launched 10 years of controversy around the future of the building.

Successive plans for redevelopment

Throughout the 1970s and 1980s there was a constant stream of complaints from residents about maintenance problems at the Brunswick. Clearly, they were unhappy about the state of the building and what was perceived as Camden Council's reluctance to maintain it. From the start, the relationship between the freeholder and the Camden housing authority had been strained, and the unconventional partnership between the two was later to result in significant disagreements about which party should shoulder responsibility for which aspects of the Brunswick's maintenance. Although it was specified in the lease that the freeholder retained responsibility for the structure of the building, it soon became clear that defining where that began and ended was not easy.

23 Gardiner, Stephen (1971). 'Not as Nature intended' *Observer Review*, 12 Dec
24 Johnstone, Violet (1972). 'Another London "Barbican", custom-built for Bloomsbury', *Daily Telegraph*, 27 Jun.
25 Kendall, Ena (1973). 'Babylon Comes to Bloomsbury'. *Observer Magazine* 2 Dec, p 33.

In 1978, *Building Design* published a very rude commentary[26] on the
Brunswick, which gave voice to a general sense of decay and decline.
Christopher Knight wrote

> *"Even in purely architectural terms the Brunswick Centre doesn't work. The supposedly cascading glass merely dribbles down in a crude flow impeded by the coarse detailing of patent glazing. The plain windows in concrete walls look mean and ill-proportioned against the massive concrete megastructure, itself never finished as intended [painted!] and consequently grim, weatherstained and repellent."*

In 1979 the residents protested that the estate had become a 'slum'. On top of all the other problems, life on the estate was seriously disrupted by undesirable intruders in the accessible public areas. Rate and rent reductions of 5% were introduced in acknowledgement of residents' complaints. In the same year, Patrick Hodgkinson then lent his name and support to a scheme by Max Hutchinson, a future President of the RIBA, to build a new floor of penthouses on top of the Brunswick, as originally conceived. This project was shelved because of costs, but in 1983, a £2 million repair scheme was put in place, which included the construction of a wall across the grand central staircase, in order to keep unwanted visitors off the terraces.

Only in 1991 were new street entrances to the two blocks finally constructed, equipped with heavy wooden doors and operated by an electronic entry system with individual fobs for residents. This significantly improved the security of the estate, although the new doors rather detracted from the integrity of the original concept. During the 1990s, further Estate Action work was carried out to the residential areas by Camden, involving the introduction of closed-circuit TV, new lighting, the removal of graffiti, and patchy concrete repairs which ultimately failed and did nothing to improve the building's appearance. Damp remained a chronic problem. Security was further improved, with the closure in 1992 of the underground service road and removal of the vagrant community there under the supervision of Tranmac, the Brunswick Outreach Team, the police, Salvation Army, Father Barry Carpenter, and the press.

However, the overall quality of the Brunswick was in steady decline. The shopping centre was looking more tawdry, unloved, and under-used than ever. According to Hodgkinson, it had been occupied from the start by 'a supermarket and a riffraff of tired traders they [the commercial letting agents] thought might suit council tenants...'[27]. And in 1991, when Rugby Estates purchased the freehold of the Brunswick from Marchmont Properties, English Heritage's London Advisory Committee[28] recorded the view that it was in a

> *"state of decline that had arisen from a gross lack of maintenance, and reduced commercial viability stemming in part from ill-defined entrances to the Centre at its main commercial connections from Bernard Street and Marchmont Street. Tranmac [set up by Rugby Estates] commissioned a market survey of public and commercial attitudes which confirmed the generally held poor*

26 Knight, Christopher (1993). 'Blast Brunswick', Letters, *Building Design* 26 Nov, quoting his own article in *Building Design* (1978).
27 Hodgkinson, P. 'Speculation with Humanity?' Architect's statement (10 July 1992) to planning authority, in response to Tranmac planning application.
28 English Heritage: London Advisory Committee, 5 Nov 1993, item 6g. The Brunswick Centre, planning application at consultation stage.

view of the Centre, its threatening image (due to the presence of numbers of vagrants in unsupervised public areas), and the large percentage of people unaware of the existence of the shopping centre, even among those living and working nearby.'

Le Riche Maw redevelopment scheme (1992)

Tranmac employed the architects Le Riche Maw to prepare a scheme **[38]** that included the sale of new housing as a route to financing long-term improvements to the shopping centre. In May 1992 they submitted a planning application for a new 7-storey building on Bernard Street, filling the open southern end of the precinct between the ends of O'Donnell and Foundling Courts, and another 8-storey building filling the space under the portico, or loggia, onto Brunswick Square. The blocks were to be constructed in brick in a traditional style, completely at odds with the appearance of the Brunswick. The scheme was heavily criticised, stimulating a request for spot-Listing of the building for its own protection, and in July Hodgkinson wrote his own response, 'Speculation with Humanity?',[27] which outlined the vexed history of the Brunswick, and condemned the proposed blocks as 'large and offensive'. At the same time he rather surprisingly resurrected the original idea of extending the building north to Tavistock Place, which had been dead and buried for 20 years, and was most unlikely to gain public support. He objected that

> *"Nothing is proposed to terminate the complex satisfactorily at Handel Street, nor, alternatively, is there any suggestion of completing the whole project to Tavistock Place, which was consented to by Camden as an imperative before my departure and to transform this seedy, unkempt 'Brutalist' ghost (I was never of that ilk) into the rich village we had once imagined, its paint and colour brought alive by summer sun and glinting from the reflection of street lamps on wet and foggy November afternoons. That, to myself and many others, I suspect, is the London we love."*

Hodgkinson was annoyed that the developers had not contacted him about the redevelopment proposals, highlighting the fact that 'unlike France, for example, Britain does not have copyright laws to protect an architect's work, as his or her work of art, from ruination'. The only way in which Hodgkinson could fight to protect his building was by lending his support to the campaign for spot-Listing, even though this might close the door to future improvements – the last thing Hodgkinson wanted was for the Brunswick to be 'frozen' as a period piece of 1960s architecture. The unique case put the whole issue of architectural copyright firmly into the public domain. As Dan Cruickshank pointed out[29] in the *Architects' Journal*,

> *"It is rare for a living and still relatively young architect to find himself promoting his own architecture as historic.... Hodgkinson has no recourse other than to present himself as a maker of historic buildings – a posture that must necessarily be somewhat painful to a life-long supporter of Modernism."*

He also stressed that *"the problem lies not with the idea of extending the Centre, only with the way that it would be done."* The article suggested that the Brunswick had already developed a rather exotic feel[29] because of the way

29 Astragal (1992). 'Kasbahs in exotic Brunswick', *Architects' Journal* 29 Jul, p 49.

individual residents had 'personalised' their balconies, and that there was no reason why the place should not be colonised, in line with Louis Kahn's idea of 'inhabited ruins' – perhaps using a lightweight architecture 'to contrast with the concrete of the main structure and to work in harmony with the original conservatories'.

After a highly public campaign, both the application for Listing and the planning application were ultimately turned down; a 5-year Certificate of Immunity from Listing was also issued. Many people were as horrified at the idea of the building being Listed as others were by the proposed scheme.

David Rock & Camp 5 redevelopment scheme (1993)

After the application had been refused, Tranmac appointed a new architect in 1993, David Rock (former President of the RIBA) with Camp 5. Rock in turn appointed Patrick Hodgkinson as consultant, but when the latter produced some preliminary sketches it quickly became clear the two parties did not see eye to eye. A new scheme was eventually submitted by Camp 5, consisting of a free-standing 12-storey 'gateway' residential building at the Brunswick Square entrance, constructed of metal, glass, hardwood and ceramic tile, and containing 50 one- to three-bedroom flats and 10 studio flats or bedsitters [39]. For security reasons, to prevent access to the podium level, the monumental external staircase to the terrace was to be removed. In addition, the parts of the terrace that connected across and overshadowed the precinct, plus their supporting columns, were to be removed and replaced by two lightweight footbridges connecting the two sides, and yellow canopies were to be installed along the middle of the 'mall' over an extension to the Safeway frontage.

This scheme was subjected to an extensive consultation process, and generated another wave of publicity in the national and architectural press. Camden's planning department received some 125 letters in response to their consultation operation, 84% of which objected, and 16% of which supported at least a part of it. These included representations from the Twentieth Century Society, Camden Civic Society, Rugby and Harpur Resident's Association, and the newly-formed Save the Brunswick Centre Group, which had organised a petition containing a remarkable 675 signatures from residents, neighbours, and from further afield. In addition, 15 letters were received from architects, rallied by Hodgkinson, unanimously rejecting the scheme both as damaging to the original design and as being out of context with the general area.

In October 1993, Hodgkinson published his own alternative scheme in *Building Design* showing how 104 new flats for sale could be constructed as a top storey, as originally conceived, arranged in clusters of 13 flats around each pair of 8 ventilation chimneys, and removing the need for a new residential building at ground level. In April 1994, the Rock/Camp 5 scheme was refused on 13 counts, and withdrawn without a formal planning application being made – despite Rock's lament that the Brunswick was 'dying'.[30] However, the removal of the staircase and podium was approved and implemented.

30 Rock, David (1993). Perspective, *Building Design*, 5 Nov, p 8.

Hawkins/Brown–Michael Squire scheme (1996)

By 1996, a third scheme had been produced, this time by architects Hawkins/Brown, who had assisted David Rock on the previous project, for the commercial areas, and Michael Squire Associates for the housing elements [40]. As Hodgkinson wrote,[31] the new scheme made exactly the same mistakes as the earlier two:

> *"All three applications have made the same gross error of infilling the Brunswick Square loggia with a "toff's" block of sanitised flats backing onto the community and harming its amenities – the worst type of social segregation from which vandalism invariably results."*

The new scheme also proposed the same extension of Safeway into the precinct that had previously been ruled unacceptable – *"it would destroy the rhythm of the colonnade which provides order to variegated shop fronts."*[31]

By this time Hodgkinson seemed to have accepted that extension of the centre northwards was out of the question, and he made the suggestion, later to be realised – by which time he was not so happy about it, and proposed putting it in the basement instead – that a better location for an enlarged supermarket would be at the north end, finally closing off the axis and 'providing an anchor' to the shopping street. He also argued that the best way of securing the Brunswick's future as a 'destination' of some quality would be by 'introducing new cultural activities to draw people from London generally that will in turn attract a better class of shop and restaurant etc.' By contrast, he said, the current proposals 'represent the tatty end of design thinking aimed at low-grade tourism'. He also questioned again whether any new housing was needed at all, reiterating the fact that the original design concept already held the potential for vertical extension, via a new top-floor storey, which could, depending on a cooperative attitude between freeholder and lessee, easily be achieved.

As for the notion of building a new block in front of the Renoir portico, he compared it to 'leaning a similar block against the Marble Arch'. He reminded his readers of the symbolic significance of the loggia, describing it as a

> *"unique instance of urban largesse that represents our socio-civic values... designed in memory of Ruskin (born on the site) and those Bloomsbury philosophers whose beliefs encouraged our social revolution...metaphorically with its seven pillars it is the equivalent of an archway ventilating today's village with the fresh air those thinkers breathed into our clogged lungs from the last century onwards."*

According to the Royal Fine Art Commission, this third scheme was the best to date, but it recommended making use of the original architect's current ideas. English Heritage, surprisingly, did not object to the application, commending the height reduction to the proposed flats, but the Twentieth Century Society remained opposed to the loss of the dramatic portal onto Brunswick Square. As for the residents, they took up arms once again, and the Council received another deluge of protests and a petition containing 202 signatures.

The proposed new block of flats was described in pejorative terms as

---

31 PH, 'Observations on the present planning application, by the original architect' 7.8.1996.

the 'lean-to' building, and residents were especially outraged at the threat these privately owned homes posed to the light and air of council tenants, regarded as adding insult to injury. Residents strongly felt they were being laid open to exploitation by a large corporation intent on squeezing profits out of the place they called home. The petition enumerated a further nine points concerning the unacceptable practical implications of the scheme, including noise and dust from construction work, the addition of canopies to the shopping arcade blocking the view of residents down into the precinct, the possibility of a wind tunnel effect through the precinct, the felling of trees on surrounding streets, the proposed change of use of flats to shops at the south end of Marchmont Street with the potential noise from delivery lorries; potential disruption from the proposed bar/café on Bernard Street, and the proposed demolition of the second floor deck, which would cut off the connection between the blocks at the south end. It was also suggested that Rugby Estates had no intention of doing any work itself, and would simply sell the property on once planning permission had been obtained. The final demand was that the freeholder should take steps to clean up the estate straight away.

The Planning Inquiry

In face of such overwhelming opposition, the council issued another rejection, and consequently, following Rugby Estates' appeal against the decision, the case went in 1997 to a Planning Inquiry, headed by Inspector Nicholas Hammans. Architectural historian and local resident Alan Powers took the opportunity to publish a candid reappraisal[32] of the Brunswick in *The Spectator* – the first new critique of substance to be published since Hamilton Eddy's 10 years previously. Powers pointed out that the development 'was an attempt to do something for the community we are all still searching for', highlighting the fact that the ideas embodied in the Brunswick might have a renewed relevance for the future of urban planning. On the other hand, he protested, 'so massively was thought embodied in concrete that you must like it or lump it', and the sense of sheer fixedness, the non-transmutable quality of the Brunswick, seemed to locate it firmly in a bygone era of architectural production. Powers also felt that the Brunswick's freedom from the car, which at the time (and no less so today) seemed such a good idea, 'was bought at a high price of disconnection from the surrounding street network.' But in counterpoint to these criticisms, his evocation of its architectural qualities was persuasive:

> *"Against the evening light, or on a winter's evening, the tall thin columns standing out against the chiaroscuro background provides one of the few genuinely sublime architectural sights of London."*

Powers' piece heralded the production of a considerable body of evidence at the Public Inquiry, and a thoroughgoing reconsideration of the Brunswick, its place in history, and its relevance for the future – culminating in the apparently modest, but significant, recommendation that there was

> *"no reason to defer cleaning, repair of surfaces and normal maintenance which would make this striking structure instantly more attractive."* [33]

---

32 Powers, Alan (1997). 'The battle of Brunswick' *The Spectator* 21 Jun, p 40.
33 Nicholas Hammans (1997). Planning Inquiry report, in English Heritage archives.

The Inspector – whom Hodgkinson described as thoughtful and sympathetic – made it clear that the long-term, inexcusable neglect of the Brunswick had played a major part in a process of degradation which was not by any means inherent to the architecture itself. At the same time, he drew attention to the fact that the proposed housing block was, in effect, a windfall site, as it was not one identified in the Unitary Development Plan for prospective housing – but it did not contain the required amount of family accommodation. Finally, the style of the block was completely wrong – 'a wholly disparate element set in a very conspicuous place', where 'the dominant theme... is the uncompromising and insistent rhythm of the Brunswick Centre.'

As for proposals for the shopping centre, the Inquiry suggested that although 'the retail Plaza is intentionally self-contained and inward looking', the introduction of new kiosks within the space 'could enliven the plaza and reduce its apparent excess width.' It pointed out that

> *"it is not designed for maximum retail efficiency. The monumental access through the loggia does not relate to the shopping streets of Bloomsbury, it relates to the park, whence few shoppers come."*

These issues were central to the concerns of the freeholder, and while rejecting Tranmac's appeal, the Inquiry seemed to open the way for the implementation of certain alterations to the public space.

The outcome of the appeal was met with mixed feelings. Safeway and Iceland, the two largest retail units in the shopping precinct, had been clamouring for an approval, fearing that the Brunswick was set to decline if no progress was made. Niyasi Eren of Ukay Hamburger Restaurant, however, wrote to the *Camden New Journal*[34], applauding the victory 'over unscrupulous speculators', which had saved the architectural integrity of the Brunswick. He took the opportunity to protest against the exorbitant rents charged by Rugby Estates, which he identified, along with a lack of proper upkeep, as the real cause of the Brunswick's decline. On 9 January 1998 Camden approved a revised version of the scheme for improvements to the shopping centre only, upon which Rugby Estates struck a deal with Allied London Properties for £13 million and sold up.

Allied London's Hodgkinson/Stubbs Rich scheme (1999)

Allied London bought the site amid much fanfare and promises that it would invest up to £3 million in an improvement scheme. The company seemed to appreciate the building's significance, describing it for *The Times* as "greatly ahead of its time"[35], and also communicated a clear idea of what a regenerated Brunswick could do to create a new focus for Bloomsbury. During 1998 local residents, shoppers, visitors and people working in the area were consulted about possible improvements, and the decision to bring Patrick Hodgkinson back on board was also a beneficial publicity move. As Michael Ingall, chief executive of Allied London, put it later:

> *"We are delighted to take him on because he is the authority on the building. His plans will give the centre a new lease of life and create a new heart for Bloomsbury."*[36]

34 Letters, *Camden New Journal*, 14 Aug 1997.
35 *The Times*, 19 Jun 1999.
36 Quoted in *Camden Chronicle* 20.2.2000, p 8.

In order to work up a scheme, Hodgkinson forged an uneasy relationship *vicissitudes* with a commercial practice, Stubbs Rich, which had an office in Bath and expertise in computer imaging. In 1999 an exhibition, mounted at the Brunswick, of a new scheme submitted for planning application, showed **[41]** a large new building filling in the northern end and a circular projection to the Renoir portico, as well as extensions of the shopping arcades into the precinct. Press reaction was extremely negative, and Hodgkinson was accused of ruining his own building. Some questioned whether he was even capable of revisiting a project he had originally designed 30 years before, since when he had scarcely practised as an architect. In a piece entitled, 'Whose building is it anyway?', the *Observer*'s architecture critic commented[37] on the bizarre situation of Hodgkinson 'having to defend his right to alter the design against conservationists who want to save him from himself', and quoted Kenneth Powell, of the Twentieth Century Society, saying

> "We don't like the way that he is proposing to monkey around with the Brunswick Centre. It's his plan for a supermarket that's the worst thing."

Hodgkinson himself admitted that

> "[the building] has been something of an embarrassment to me over the years, but this gives me the chance to put it right",[38]

and he rejected the suggestion that he might not be up to the task.

The conservationists' concerns won. They were upset not only by the supermarket, but by the proposed alterations to the Renoir portico and the plan to introduce a glazed restaurant structure in the precinct. After much dissent, to which the Bloomsbury Conservation Area Advisory Committee lent its voice, disaster struck when, after submission and approval of a new scheme in 2000, the building was finally Listed in September 2000, and the planning approval thereby nullified. The whole process, it seemed, would have to be relaunched. By this time residents were close to despair, especially as none of the routine maintenance and cleaning work recommended by the Inquiry had been implemented.

Listing of the Brunswick (achieved 2000)

Allied London was furious when the Twentieth Century Society resurrected its campaign to have the Brunswick Listed, at the end of the 5-year certificate of immunity, and so was Patrick Hodgkinson, in his new role as architect to the improvement scheme. Apart from anything else, the case for Listing made great play with the notion of the Brunswick as a megastructure. A new article in *The Guardian*'s 'Space' supplement[39] defined the project as "one of the first and best examples of megastructures", and even referenced Archigram and Peter Cook's Plug-In City, both anathema to Hodgkinson.

Camden too was unhappy about Listing, fearing a huge escalation of its management and maintenance costs. Local Councillor Brian Weekes warned in doom-laden terms[40] that Listing would be a 'catastrophe', making redeveloping the Brunswick far more expensive, so that the building would

---

37 Deyan Sudjic (2000). Whose building is it anyway? *Observer Review*, 19 Mar.
38 Hodgkinson, P (2000). *Camden Chronicle*, 20 Feb, p 8.
39 Kerr, Joe (2000). 'Big is Beautiful'. In 'Space', *The Guardian*, 4 May, pp 13-14.
40 Brian Weekes, interview with the author, 2000.

probably be sold again to some overseas developer who would simply allow it to deteriorate to a point where Camden would give permission for them to do anything they wanted, including demolition. The Listing process was also resisted by DOCOMOMO on the grounds that the whole point of a megastructure was that it could grow and adapt over time and not be frozen, but the bandwagon had gathered momentum, and the decision seemed almost a foregone conclusion after the trial run of 1992. English Heritage had launched a concerted effort to secure the recognition and Listing of significant post-war buildings, and the Brunswick, along with Charles Holden's Underground stations, Basil Spence's Swiss Cottage Library and Lasdun's Institute of Education building were among those identified in north and east London. Furthermore, EH was currently carrying out its Heritage Review, with a view to updating the whole concept of 'heritage' and embracing more of the social context of architecture than before. The Brunswick was regarded as an architectural 'icon' that could also be read as a vivid document of the recent social history of the area.[41]

Levitt Bernstein with Patrick Hodgkinson scheme (2002)

English Heritage made it clear that the Listing of the building should not be seen as precluding the refurbishment of the Brunswick, and pointed out that listing as Grade II rather than Grade II* acknowledged both the previous structural alterations and the possibility of future improvements. It also stressed that the first scheme submitted by Allied London was not acceptable. The developer responded by immediately replacing Stubbs Rich by Levitt Bernstein, the successful specialist housing practice founded by Hodgkinson's original assistants on the Brunswick, David Levitt and David Bernstein. The structural engineering consultant was Buro Happold. Hodgkinson himself had already made clear his unhappiness with the Stubbs Rich scheme, but was happy to work with Levitt Bernstein on a new scheme, prepared in consultation with English Heritage.

This was again greeted with raised eyebrows in many quarters, and flatly opposed by the local Conservation Area Committee as being out of character both with the Brunswick and its surroundings, largely on the grounds of the proposed alterations to the Renoir portico. The Planning Committee was not enraptured with it either, but was prepared to go along with it to prevent further deterioration. However, only one objection was received from residents, whose reception of the latest proposals were generally positive – as well they might be, because by this time the fear that the building might fall into irreversible disrepair, and even the possibility of demolition, had become palpable.

The Levitt Bernstein–Hodgkinson scheme [42] submitted for Listed Building Consent in May 2001, and finally approved in September 2003, featured most prominently a large circular 'eye-catcher' structure underneath, and projecting from, the Renoir portico towards Brunswick Square which was intended to be a restaurant or café, drawing attention to the centre as a shopping and leisure destination. Allied London was considering introducing new cultural attractions, the British Cartoon Gallery, and possibly a large

41 Kevin Murphy, English Heritage caseworker, interviewed by author 5 Dec 2000.

bookshop, catering for the academic residents and students in the area,
but the consensus was that the most valuable draw to the Brunswick had
historically been, and would be, a large supermarket.

The residents of the Brunswick were largely in favour of the scheme, but
they were also anxious to be involved in discussions with the freeholder, and
to ensure that prospective improvements would not be confined solely to the
shopping centre but also deliver benefits to the inhabitants of the housing
above it. They felt both possessive about their territory and exasperated
by the lack of feedback on the continuing maintenance problems they had
suffered from for so long. The Tenants and Residents' Association, under
the chairmanship of Stuart Tappin, a structural engineer by profession,
had initiated a campaign to be involved in talks with Allied London and
the architects which would allow them to put forward their views, although
Allied London made it clear from the outset that, strictly speaking, they
owed the residents nothing. In 2004, in the announcement of an imminent
start on the works, at a cost of £22 million, the developer's spokesman Neil
Carron stressed that the new Brunswick was

> "designed to be a neighbourhood area for Bloomsbury – not just for the tenants
> who live above the shops." [42]

At this point, plans for the semicircular restaurant had been temporarily
shelved, attention being focused on the construction of the new supermarket
building, painting and fresh landscaping of the hard surfaces, and
improvements to the retail units that would ensure take-up by 'big-name'
retailers. 'Centre' had finally been dropped from the name, along with the
concept of the 'precinct', and the development had been re-branded as 'the
Brunswick, a high street for Bloomsbury', adorned with works by the artist
Susanna Heron. The residents and tenants were pleased, but retained some
suspicion of the project. As Tappin said, they were

> "really keen for work to start. We are trying to make sure that the residents
> have a voice in the changes that are being made. But for some of us it's a
> shame that we are going to have High Street chains like Starbucks rather
> than a more interesting mix..."

For Hodgkinson, the key point was that at last the building would have
its finishing coat of paint: "*When it's painted cream I hope it will look like the
terraces by Regent's Park*", he said, adding "*I can see it going the way of the
Barbican*" as an upmarket mixed-use development with a strong cultural
focus.

Early in 2005, this hope received a further fillip when it was revealed that
Waitrose was to step in to replace Safeway as supermarket anchor to the site.
After 30 years at the Brunswick, Safeway, which had recently been taken
over by Morrisons, had announced its lack of interest in retaining a shop
there, causing a moment of crisis in the progress towards implementation
of works. But its replacement was widely welcomed. To quote the chief
executive of Allied London,

> "It is exactly the type of offer Bloomsbury needs and wants. We chose Waitrose
> because of its proven ability to attract and perform in this sort of central
> London location." [43]

42 Janssen, Kim (2004). 'Will Brunswick shine brightly 45 years on?' *Camden New Journal* 15 Jul.
43 Spittles, David (2005). Bloomsbury moves up in the world. *Evening Standard* 7 Feb, p 84.

The 'Waitrose factor' was hailed as the linchpin of the Brunswick's future success, providing the catalyst for the arrival of other reputable, upmarket traders, with a knock-on effect for the whole future of Bloomsbury.

Not exactly the cultural centre Hodgkinson had dreamt of, but potentially a magnet for the sort of customers who might be interested in using the revamped Renoir art house cinema. At a party held to launch the works in May of 2005, it was suggested[44] by the chief executive of the news organisation ITN, based in nearby Gray's Inn Road, that the successful regeneration of the Brunswick as a shopping centre could attract an influx of media companies into the area, turning Bloomsbury into 'a media centre to rival Canary Wharf and Soho', for it was only the lack of good-quality shopping that was keeping companies away. The only, barely-heard, voice of dissent came from those residents of the Brunswick who lamented the loss of Safeways as an old friend and complained that they would not be able to afford Waitrose prices, but by this time the excitement and publicity around impending operations was loud enough to drown it out. Work finally began in 2005.

44 Janssen, Kim (2005). Centre revamp 'could lure media'. *Camden New Journal* 5 May, p 12.

4 Inside looking out: the residents' story

Illustrations numbered in square brackets are shown on pp 96 ff.

Unless indicated, quotations from residents are from interviews with the author in 2000-1 and 2004-6

Looking back to the days when the first residents moved in to the Brunswick, Sue Kensdale, chair of the Tenants' Association, said in 1990 *"It was an honour to live here, as it was a very elegant block. We thought it was paradise, but now it's gone to pot."* By that time, residents had been demanding action from the council for nearly two decades on matters including rubbish disposal, damp, security, concrete repairs and heating, all the while witnessing a steady decline of the shopping centre under their homes. During the 1990s, they found themselves in an increasingly confrontational situation with the freeholder, as successive schemes for redevelopment were advanced and rejected, and there was a growing sense that the building, as an architectural entity and as a commercial proposition, had become more important to those with a say in its future than the people who lived in it. Many of them felt a strong sense of attachment to the Brunswick as the physical framework of their daily lives and the place they called home. When it came to the question 'Whose Brunswick is it, anyway?', the answer was far from clear. The architect Patrick Hodgkinson relates a chance encounter outside the building. As he gazed up at his troubled work, an elderly Brunswick resident, Roman Malynowski, asked him

"Are you admiring my building?"

"Well yes, I'm also admiring my building!"

As Hodgkinson says,

"No architect could have asked for more: 'ownership' of a home we love is natural." [1]

Inside the Brunswick

At first it was easy to enter the two housing blocks of the Brunswick, designed as they were with open access to the staircases and with lifts at either end of each side. The idea was that the staggered access decks would form a kind of continuum with the central public street, despite being raised above it, with the numbering system organised in vertical blocks rather than continuous linear stretches, and that the blocks would have a certain permeability to the public realm. The grand staircase, clearly visible through the Brunswick Square portal [5], was intended as an expressive architectural gesture emphasising a direct route from street level up to front doors at terrace level and above. As a result, residents became used to the appearance of architecture students and curious visitors roaming the access galleries with cameras, snapping the dramatic vista through the A-frame structure (see frontispiece). They would drift past their kitchen windows, sometimes peering in to get a glimpse of the interiors.

Once the street-level doors and security system were put in place, as

---

1 Hodgkinson, Patrick (2000) 'Brunswick Centre, Bloomsbury: A Good Bit of City?' *Twentieth Century Society Journal* No. 6, pp 81-90.

a response to the problems posed by intruders, the blocks became less welcoming to visitors. Not that they became totally impermeable to the world outside, for it was still quite easy to slip inside following someone's entrance or exit, either from the street or from the precinct (via the two staircases, known as 'the back stairs', which remained open near the Safeway store). It was even possible to enter via the less conventional route of the ramps at the Bernard Street end of the building. So, although in the mid-1990s the destruction of the monumental public staircase to the second-floor terrace from the precinct seemed to draw more tightly the boundaries between public and private space and activities, they were never rigidly delineated, and the building retained a sense of connection with the life of the street. Noisy local kids messing around on the terraces, or rough sleepers, alcoholics and drug addicts using the space as a convenient shelter, continued to be a source of discontent.

Nevertheless, the interior of the housing blocks constitutes a world contrasting with that of the shopping precinct down below: the internal atrium, above which the access galleries seem to be suspended, is monumental, grand and raw, and the sheer volume, and apparent emptiness, of the space is almost overwhelming. It might be compared to a medieval cathedral, or a forest of ancient trees. For one writer, David Hamilton Eddy, it is a slightly uncomfortable experience: *"we feel the anxieties of being naked."* [2] A visitor can feel exposed, surveyed by potentially hundreds of eyes through the small kitchen windows that look out over the extremely long access galleries. One resident, French-born Isabelle Chaise, says she always sees the route to her front door as a long perspective viewed through a camera lens and has the disconcerting sensation of being viewed through such a lens while she traverses the access galleries.

Furthermore, as one resident explains, it is impossible to have a private conversation anywhere within the atrium because of the way sound is carried and amplified. For some tenants and residents, the route to their front door passes through an environment they would more readily term 'a concrete jungle' than anything else. One elderly sheltered tenant says he 'thought it was like a prison', with *"big ugly blinking walls: they should knock down the flats and put glass in and turn it into a monkey house!"* The supervisor caretaker, Frank Murphy, is not alone in his use of the epithet 'Alcatraz'; nevertheless, he was one of the people who circulated the residents' petition against Tranmac's redevelopment proposals which threatened to compromise the original appearance of the Brunswick.

Reyner Banham commented in 1976 that the Brunswick was
"seemingly the best-liked [of English megastructures] by its inhabitants, in spite of numerous vicissitudes." [3]
Although some outsiders had criticisms of its scale and its lack of detail (for despite Hodgkinson's admiration of the People's Detailing, there wasn't much of it to be seen here at the end of the convoluted procurement process), the residents seemed to like it still, 20 years on. The planning consultation generated a sack of letters from residents and business tenants, united in protesting against the redevelopment proposals. One resident,

2 Hamilton Eddy, David (1989). Castle Mythology in British Housing. *RIBA Journal* (Dec), p 31.
3 Banham, Reyner (1976). *Megastructure*. Thames & Hudson, London.

Carol Archer, subsequently described this period, the 'fight-back' against
the developers, as one of the most wonderful things in her life, and the
Brunswick as *"one of the most wonderful pieces of architecture"*. Roman
Malynowsky, the tenant whom Hodgkinson encountered outside the building
and who entered into a correspondence with him about its future, noted that

> *"its open space piazza style has no match anywhere in the borough except*
> *perhaps for the British Museum* [this was before it was converted into the
> Great Court!], *and ought to be preserved for posterity"*.

In similar vein, another letter described *"an estate of concentrated housing*
which nevertheless retains a sense of space", while a circular organised by
residents declared *"It outshines any building for miles around"*. The business
residents' letter, signed by Britannia Catering, Drury Porter Eyecare,
Femina, Hair Centre, Holland & Barrett, Marc Jason Shoeworld, and
Quality Shoe Repairs, all tenants of the 'mall' leading from the precinct into
Marchmont Street, pronounced the proposed new flats *"out of sympathy*
with the architectural vision of the Centre". Mr Eren, of Ukay Hamburger
Restaurant, in the main precinct, also representing the Shop and Offices
Tenants' Association, launched an appeal to 'Save the Colonnades!',
and warned that the developer would be counting on wearing down the
opposition to the point of capitulation. An architect resident, Brendan
Woods, described it as 'an innovative urban building'. Other voices called it
'a very pleasant place to live', and 'a most wonderful fine building', asking
"where else is there such architecture? – only here."

In 1992, Patrick Hodgkinson was approached personally by two
Brunswick residents seeking to alert him to the first planning proposal for
new blocks on Bernard Street and in front of the Brunswick Square portal.
One letter described the present blocks as *"very beautiful pieces of architecture*
to live in", and expressed the hope that Hodgkinson might be able to
advise the developers on any future redevelopment. The second, written
by Malynowsky, styling himself 'a mere tenant', deplored the fact that
Brunswick Centre was

> *"about to be devastated by a proposal before the council to build over every*
> *available square inch of space and thus destroy the whole much-loved and*
> *world-famed design"*,

referring in particular to the 'lovely eastern side'. Malynowski asked whether
Hodgkinson might be able to give advice or support to residents on *"how*
to fend off these outrageous plans". Hodgkinson responded by sending copies
of the letters to English Heritage and requesting a meeting with the Chief
Listing Officer to discuss the possibility of spot-Listing, which he saw as an
(undesirable) necessity in the circumstances.

But when the Brunswick was finally Listed, with the aim of preserving
its architectural vision for posterity, residents didn't understand. As one
said, *"It's very strange – something you do with old buildings, like Buckingham*
Palace". It just didn't seem to make sense, when for many residents the
whole point of living at the Brunswick was to benefit from its modern design
features, distinguishing it from neighbouring estates like those built by
the Peabody Trust, with their high brick-built walls, introverted courtyard
layouts, small windows and small rooms. For another resident, Listing was a
pointless exercise, simply because it happened too late:

> *"They should not have listed this building … Its best points have been*
> *shattered… the monumental staircase, the podium bridge, those are the*

highlights of this block, and by the time they Listed, those had gone! So I think that was really quite ridiculous. But I suppose the Bloomsbury Society [sic] would have their way."

Above all, the news of Listing filled many residents with dread that the longed-for repairs and improvements to the Brunswick would not take place, and the place would continue to decline steadily – even to the point, as Councillor Brian Weekes had warned, where the building might in the end have to be demolished. Most people had responded to the sale to Allied London with enthusiasm, believing that something positive would come out of it for the Brunswick: *"When Allied London bought the building it was really quite exciting"*, but it seemed that Listing would greatly increase the costs of redevelopment, making the project much less appealing to any freeholder. As another person pointed out, the 1930s Isokon building in Hampstead had been 'left to rot' after being Listed, and its future hung in the balance for a long time before it was regenerated.

At a meeting with residents in 2000, Kevin Murphy, Historic Buildings Adviser to English Heritage, stressed that the Listing of a building did not mean it could not be altered, and that English Heritage had nothing against regeneration of the Brunswick, nor with the outline intentions of Allied London and the architect, only with the lack of detail provided. Residents agreed that the Allied London scheme was the first they had been able to contemplate, although there was considerable opposition to the idea of filling in the north end of the precinct with a new supermarket building. There was a growing acceptance that Listing was not the disaster some had been led to believe; in fact it offered an opportunity for residents to become more engaged in discussions about the future of the building, by opening up new channels of communication between the different parties involved.

Early residents' views

For many people living at the Brunswick, the distinctive modern character of its design had been a primary reason for moving in. Many who have been residents from the start vividly recall the impression it made when they were first offered the opportunity of living there. Despite strong opposition in the local press to the clearance and redevelopment of the site, it seems that the new building aroused a sense of excitement locally. As the *Daily Telegraph* reported in 1972[4], the first tenants to move in that year *"find it provides a sense of identity: it's not a question of just living in another block"*. Likewise, the *Observer Magazine* reported in 1973[5] that tenants saw the Brunswick in a more positive light than other council estates:

> *Cab-driver John Lee and his wife, Wendy, who is secretary of the Tenants' Association, [say] "At first we were undecided whether to stay. Now I don't want to leave. Everyone here prefers it to a tower block and most prefer it to the normal council estate."* [5]

To be sure, not everyone felt this way. During construction, graffiti were daubed on the site hoardings, dubbing the project the 'Bloomsbury Prison', and in 2000 Professor Eric Ayers recalled in a letter to *The Guardian*[6],

4 Johnstone, Violet (1972). 'Another London Barbican, custom-built for Bloomsbury', *Daily Telegraph* 27 Jun.
5 Kendall, Ena (1973). 'Babylon comes to Bloomsbury'. *Observer Magazine* 2 Dec, p 33.
6 Ayers, Eric (2000). 'How to design housing worth living in'. Letters, *The Guardian*, 12 May, p 23.

"We watched the Brunswick Centre being built, and instantly christened it 'Planet of the Apes'. Everyone still refers to it as such. Alas, [Hodgkinson] destroyed the 'Latin Quarter' of Bloomsbury. Marchmont Street did have a real 'quartier' feel to it and it was a pleasure to shop there. But now... the centre overwhelms human beings."

But it was, and still is, outsiders who voice the most vehement dislike of the Brunswick. The first generation of residents at the Brunswick came predominantly from nearby; they had been born and brought up on or near the site or in Covent Garden, had watched the building being erected, and in many cases had specifically requested to be rehoused in the new flats, once it became clear they were not in private ownership, even though the rent, at £11 a week, was considered high.

Although there was widespread dislike of the concrete, which almost from the start showed signs of the damp that was to become such a problem, and a certain lack of enthusiasm for the common parts, where the increasingly dank and stained concrete structure had an overpowering impact, the flats themselves were almost universally considered beautiful, and indeed luxurious. As someone said at the tenants' meeting with English Heritage in 2000: *"compared to Somers Town, [the Brunswick's] a luxury pad!"* A long-standing resident recalls, of her first impressions, *"I thought it was a concrete jungle – all the red doors – but inside the flats were beautiful"*. Another remembers

"I actually thought they'd knocked two flats into one... big, big, vast it seemed.....And when I looked at the balcony, I thought, good Lord, that's quite something. You can certainly express yourself in a room this size, if you can't there's something wrong with you...And I've loved every minute of being here."

For this resident, the flat was 'fabulous', and the building overall 'should have been a showpiece', if it had been properly kept up;

"at the beginning, it was a showpiece – people used to come, and years ago when we didn't have the entry, people could walk through. I've often been sitting out on my balcony, and you'd hear someone say, my goodness, you'd never have thought it would you, coming off the main road. And then I looked over one day, and this man asked how do you get to live here?"

A third resident says

"there are a lot of problems living in a concrete block [and] if I'd been aware then what it was like...I'd probably have opted for something more traditional."

When offered the chance of moving to the Brunswick from a nearby street, she thought it looked like 'an interesting block', and anything else would have been 'less trendy, less exciting in some ways.' She agrees that visitors find the entrance and route to the flat 'a little bit alarming... the concrete and stuff', but 'they usually like this flat, they say how nice it is.' Caretaker Frank Murphy tells the same story:

"There's a very good response when [visitors] come in the door, they go, my god, wow...when you look out there you just see people in the distance.... They're quite impressed."

The balconies and 'greenhouses', providing such an open aspect to the flats, were a significant attraction to many incomers, and residents' attitudes remain generally positive. For one inhabitant, the flats evoke a 'Spanish sort of terrace type situation, a garden situation', while another describes 'a holiday feel' which belies the central, inner-city location. Frank Murphy admits he's 'never loved [the Brunswick], indeed finds it hideous', but thinks that once the refurbishment is finished,

> *"it'll look really nice, quite continental...like a Greek island, there'll be plants everywhere".*

One old lady is said to have filled her greenhouse with earth to create a bower planted with almost tree-sized plants, where she slept. A perhaps surprising fact is that the Brunswick was widely perceived as being a green and leafy place to live, despite the council's failure to implement the planting scheme designed by Hodgkinson and his team. Although one resident lamented, in her letter of objection to the redevelopment plans, the loss of 'the back gardens of a row of wonderful strong houses' and their 'virgin garden soils', another, whose early childhood was spent in the countryside, explains that she opted to live at the Brunswick precisely because of the direct access to green space it offered. The attention many inhabitants gave to the 'greening' of their balconies gives the strapline 'Babylon Comes to Bloomsbury' used in the *Observer*'s early feature[5] – the sense of hanging gardens rather than of a ziggurat temple structure.

For some people, however, the balconies and greenhouses do not work well. A couple of residents comment that, as on the access galleries, it is impossible to have a private conversation on the balconies – everything can be overheard. It is even reported that the broadcaster Jimmy Savile came to the Brunswick to consider moving in, but was put off by the lack of privacy caused by the balconies. Neighbours also tended to object to the sound of children playing there. And the wide view of the terraces opposite, with the sky above – the Futurist dimension of the design intended by the architect to lift residents above the banality of their immediate surroundings – does not suit everyone. One resident says she's *"not convinced I like the view"*, and *"I don't want forever to be thinking about it"*. A number of others stress, by contrast, the importance of the view down into the precinct from the balconies, because, as Carol Archer wrote in her letter of objection to plans to build canopies extending from the shop fronts, 'the view down humanises me and other tenants as we can see people wandering around.'

Upstairs, downstairs

At the outset, the Brunswick represented a near-unique experiment in breaking the zoning regulations that ensured clear separation between retail, office and housing in new developments. It established a model for mixed-use development embodying what was subsequently described as an 'upstairs downstairs' relationship. While this posed its own particular problems, it seemed early on that the experiment was succeeding. The shopping centre was in fairly good shape, with some 80 commercial units in occupation.

> *"When I first came here it was already quite a busy shopping centre... thriving...I just witnessed its deterioration...and I'd like to see it going back to being flourishing again",*

says one inhabitant. In 1976, the *St Pancras Chronicle* ran a feature on the Brunswick entitled 'Brunswick Centre thriving among the Regency splendour', implying that mixed-use development had a positive future. Even in that article there were indications of problems for the future. It quoted Max Filz, of Ravell's gym, as saying *"Not many people have yet discovered its existence, which is surprising."* The 'invisibility' factor was to be a significant obstacle to the continuing success of the centre as a 'shopping destination', and the high-profile re-branding of the Brunswick as 'the high street for Bloomsbury' by Allied London has been a key tactic in their strategy to reverse the situation. But the *Chronicle* also quoted Victor Bahar, 27, from Turkey, running a men's clothiers called Victor's, who described the Brunswick as 'a young people's place'. This sounded positive, but during the following years, young people misbehaving in the Brunswick, particularly on the terraces, was to become a thorn in the flesh of local residents, and remains a concern today despite the enhanced security provided by Camden council, and promised by Allied London for the future.

There were other problems in the relationship between the shopping centre, its public space, and the housing 'upstairs', with a small amount of council-owned studio-office accommodation sandwiched between them with its associated terrace area. When Allied London bought the freehold, residents made it clear they considered the company had a moral obligation not only to consider ways of enhancing the prospects of the commercial enterprises but to consult residential tenants on plans for upgrading and refurbishing the building. There was a strong feeling that the precinct and its shops were primarily to serve residents' needs, a view significantly at odds with that of the developer.

Safeway, in particular, not only represented a well-used space for meeting and talking, as well as shopping, but also offered employment opportunities, and an almost paternal presence:

> *"People knew the staff, got to know the managers, just went in to complain to the managers. It felt quite familiar on that level. We used to have jumble sales here years ago, to raise money for the tenants' association. We had them outside Safeways, and Safeways would make a contribution",*

explains caretaker Frank Murphy. For the home-carers who helped look after residents of the 200-odd sheltered flats at the Brunswick, the supermarket was vitally convenient when it came to shopping for their vulnerable clients. When news came of the closure of Safeway (by then Morrisons) and future replacement by Waitrose, many residents were unenthusiastic about the prospect of 'upmarket' shopping on their doorstep: it did not fit their image of the Brunswick as 'home'.

But for Allied London and its predecessor, the public and commercial space of the Brunswick represented much less a matter of local and domestic identity than a site of engagement with a broader community of users, including tourists, students, office workers and commuters. Their perception of the Brunswick was a resurrection of the original intention of the development as a grand, formal axis and public space between nodes of mass transport. Their sense of commitment to the welfare of council tenants is restricted to their responsibility as freeholders for maintaining the structure of the building, which has throughout been subject to complex negotiations and conflict with Camden Council. The tense relationship between the expectations of 'upstairs' and 'downstairs' has created a tangle of physical and social problems during the Brunswick's history.

Domestic issues at the Brunswick

According to the former Estate Manager June Foskett, nobody else would take on the job when she did. She came from neighbouring 'Tybald', and before that had been at the Bourne Estate in Holborn. Tybalds Close, designed in the 1960s, she considered 'very well-designed', primarily because it offered a range of flats of different sizes, so that people could remain there throughout their life and sustain strong family connections. This in turn meant that the council's social services department didn't have to invest as much money in home help. By contrast, she considered the Brunswick poorly designed because of the absence of flats with more than two bedrooms. Many of the first generation of families were obliged to move away when they outgrew the flats, some enjoying the profits made through right-to-buy and after the 1980s. Others had stayed, but were effectively stuck in inappropriate accommodation, with no prospect of being rehoused because of the council's statutory obligation to give priority to homeless families who may have come into the borough from outside. This caused considerable resentment.

Apart from the planning drawbacks, the Brunswick's 'very bad reputation' for maintenance put people off. It was attributed partly to the problems of the leasehold agreement, partly to the design itself. Water seeps, very visibly, through the walls of some flats, and before refurbishment work started, the structure and surfaces of the Brunswick were badly blemished by holes and stains. In some places bits of rusty reinforcement metal had started to show through the surfaces. The concrete looked dreadful, and most residents hated it, repeatedly calling for it to be painted, in many cases taking matters into their own hands and painting their own small sections of façade, flouting council restrictions. This paintwork in turn began to decay and peel, adding to the overall sad appearance of the building only a feeling of the residents' determination to establish a personal sense of home within the 'concrete jungle'.

The expansion joints became a problem because of the heat generated in the blocks by solar glare through the greenhouses. Water accumulated on the terraces, which have now been repaired and paved with shining Chinese granite, 'like swimming pools'. The single glazing to the greenhouses generated condensation. A strong sense of the building's decaying, leaky, exposed and vulnerable fabric pervaded occupants' everyday experience of living at the Brunswick. The building has a strange, musty smell when you come in, comments one resident, who didn't use her hot-air heating system for two years because she was convinced the air coming out of it was bad. There have been serious problems with the heating, despite the installation of new boilers in 1999. The celebrated hot-air, otherwise known as 'blow-out', system (in bays 1 and 1a: bay 2, at the northern end, was built with a conventional radiator system instead) was what prompted the decision, when the Brunswick was built, to make extensive sheltered housing provision here for elderly and frail tenants – but, says a warden, it has seriously affected tenants with chronic airway disease. Acoustically, there are curious problems with the building. Sound travels by unexpected routes through the structure, throwing residents into unwelcome proximity with strangers and their activities, for instance shouting and fighting, with no evidence of its source. More bizarrely, one inhabitant used to hear the sound of bells jingling around the feet of a belly dancer in an Indian restaurant that once operated in the precinct.

According to one source, the Council is simply unable to maintain a
block of this design. Another states

> *"There was a lot of anger when I moved in and it comes from the fact that Camden didn't keep their side of the bargain [with the freeholder] and do the maintenance...the block was in bad condition for 20 years, and terrible condition for 12."*

During the 1990s the Tenants and Residents' Association, which held its first meeting under the chairmanship of Nicola Seyd to discuss the use of the noisy rubbish chutes, was resurrected, after a period in hibernation, to deal with maintenance issues as a matter of urgency. Camden took legal action to establish the freeholder's responsibilities, but lost its case. In addition to all the fabric repairs required, the blocks urgently needed rewiring. Asbestos was found in the ceilings, so lighting to the access galleries at ground and first floor level could not be upgraded. In 2000, the council took the Brunswick off its major works programme because, it said, it was the responsibility of the owner. The residents were in despair. Finally, by 2004, Camden council and Allied London managed to reach an agreement on repairs whereby the council committed itself to repairing and replacing the window frames and glazing of the flats, using self-cleaning solar-protected glass, re-laying drains on the balconies and re-paving the surfaces, and addressing the damp problems, while Allied London undertook to sort out the problems of expansion joints and the associated water penetration, along with the cleaning and painting of the exterior façades and the A-frame structure of the internal atrium. This was the programme of work started by the freeholder in 2005; Camden lagged behind, to residents' annoyance, but promised to meet its responsibilities in a subsequent phase of work.

At the same time, Camden had opened negotiations over replacing the hot-air heating system with a radiator system, which was controversial because of the potential costs to be shouldered by leaseholders, but nonetheless overdue and welcome for that reason. All in all, by 2005, despite the complaints of residents about the lack of synchronisation in the work, the massive disruption to everyday life, and the expense of shopping in Waitrose, the Brunswick's future was looking more promising, and there was talk of a dramatic increase in its desirability. Vicky Richardson, a resident for 5 years, editor of *Blueprint* design magazine, and daughter of Hodgkinson's assistant on the Brunswick, Tony Richardson, says *"Finally, we're going up in the world ...already flats in the Brunswick are hard to come by."* [7]

Life at the Brunswick had not been all bad in the past. At the outset, the housing opportunities it offered were highly regarded. One resident recalls that the area housing office *"used to vet people to move into this prestige development"*. It was seen as very desirable:

> *"There's definitely a hierarchy within the system – the difference between living on a sink estate and living in the Brunswick"*, while *"Peabody* [round the corner] *is definitely not class!"*

However, the nickname 'Brunswick Hilton' actually gained currency as an ironic reference to the subterranean community of homeless vagrants and alcoholics who were finally evicted in 1992, and had a serious negative impact on the early reputation of the Brunswick. The lifting of the precinct

7 Richardson, Vicky (2006). Brunswick Centre Bliss. *Time Out*, 1-8 Feb, p 150.

above street level had been driven by the need to accommodate extensive car parking, service access, and plant in two basements. These two storeys of damp, artificially lit space, hidden from public view, were to become intimately familiar to Site Superintendent Sid Towner, who described the unwelcome inhabitants of the area.[8]

As early as 1975, prostitutes were plying their trade in the two car parks and service road area. By 1977 it had become a meeting point for vagrants who would buy alcohol in Safeways and consume it in the precinct, or, if raining, down below. The closure of hostels and mental institutions in north London in the 1980s led to an influx of homeless people onto the streets, and the Brunswick offered an appealing refuge in the Holborn area. At one time there were as many as 57 people occupying the service road, and 10 in one plant room. "There was a sort of structure to it in the early years. The drunks would occupy the east side of the service road, and the homeless the west: there were special benefits on the east side, including hot air from the Safeway freezer extract, and fire hoses to shower under and wash their clothes: the clothing was then hung up to dry under the hot air."

During the 1980s, the existing community was augmented by drug users, with consequent increasing levels of violence and aggression, various attempted murder charges, and a steady encroachment into the whole labyrinthine basement area. Towner again:

> "To the north end of the precinct we have an area known as the void. This area was entered by knocking down two walls, they pulled out all the lighting and fouled the whole area. After being evicted from the void they broke into switch rooms, plant rooms (etc)....While in the rooms they turned off extraction and supply plant, pulled fuses out and broke light fittings, which was not only dangerous for them but also dangerous for the people that lived and worked at the centre."

The whole situation was out of control, and after lengthy negotiations between Tranmac, the police, various agencies concerned with the welfare of the homeless, and the Tenants' Association, a date was finally fixed (7 December 1992) for the eviction of all the unofficial residents of the Brunswick, which was successfully completed.

Even after 1992, security problems in the housing blocks and the ongoing problem of repairs at the Brunswick made it hard to reinstate a positive image for the building. Nevertheless, one resident says *"even now you get people saying, oh, I would love to live round there, I'd really love to."* Although some of the long-term residents had chosen to buy their flats at a generous discount in the 1980s (the price was £17,000), sell up and move away because they could not accommodate a family in two bedrooms, others, especially those who had grown up in the area and had strong local family and social ties, resented having to make that choice. Others again, who bought and stayed, eventually sold back to the council when they found they were unable to afford the service and maintenance charges and ongoing costs of home ownership.

As one tenant observes,

> "When I came on the estate first [1991] there were quite a lot of extended families. Lots of them....If you brought your kids up on the estate and they were getting married you'd go down to the local housing office, and

---

8 Towner, Sid, from his notes.

get a flat...I think it's gone to the other extreme, families are completely *living there*
broken up...the only people getting flats...have been in prison, have alcohol
problems...or are young offenders".

There is a sense that the Council's statutory obligation to give priority
to the homeless, whether 'offenders' of one sort or another, or refugees,
or simply people 'who don't come from London', has disadvantaged local
residents.

The early sense of the Brunswick's desirability was founded primarily on
the size and brightness of the flats and their balconies [43], even though they
were less generous than intended and the brightness could turn to solar glare
on one side while the entrance hall and kitchen tended to be unlit, gloomy
spaces. The kitchen was really too small for a family to eat in, and some
people disliked the lack of separation between kitchen and living room. This
led some occupants to extend the partition wall to the ceiling or to install
glazing, so that someone working in the kitchen could still supervise children
playing in the living room. According to one tenant, 'Most people thought
the kitchen should be a bit bigger and the front room smaller', a view in
tune with the design approach used by Hodgkinson in his earlier Brixton
and St Pancras schemes. But, as he had commented when the Brunswick
opened, 'people living there must be urbanites',[4 (p 62)] the presumption
being that they would not spend much time at home: more like 'our young
professionals', as one resident put it. During the 1990s the first generation of
tenants who had exercised their right to buy their flats began to sell them to
youthful, design-conscious enthusiasts who (according to the same tenant)
would have the 'level of education and aesthetic sense' to appreciate living in
the building.

The 'stunning appearance' of the Brunswick or the 'striking geometry'
of the A-frame structure may have attracted some newcomers, but for
others it was the peace and quiet offered by the location despite being in the
heart of the capital. Or because 'there was somewhere to store the bicycles'
– besides the additional balcony space, tenants can also rent a generous store
cupboard on the first floor at a small weekly charge. According to structural
engineer Stuart Tappin, who became chair of the Tenants' Association not
long after moving in,

> "People thought we were outsiders who were just interested in the reputation of
> the building and not in the people who lived here."

He has established his credentials through five years' widely appreciated
hard work representing the residents' interests, while others among the
'young professionals' have now established their own young families at
the Brunswick. They show a certain tenacity in hanging on to their central
London homes, though the regeneration of the Brunswick could increase
the value of their flats to the point where the temptation to move becomes
irresistible. Some of the current residents are shown on p 97 ([44]).

Children and neighbours

At the beginning, says one resident, there was 'a lot of trouble with children'.
Although there were only 11 or 12 children at the Brunswick at first, and by
1985 very few indeed, there was constant dispute over whether they should
be allowed to play on the terraces or not. Hodgkinson's original scheme had
included play areas in some of the covered circulation spaces connecting the

internal walkway and the terrace, but they had never been implemented. The terraces were directly overlooked by one-bedroom and studio flats occupied by single people or childless couples, for whom the noise of cycling, roller-skating, and shouting up to parents on the upper floors could be very disturbing. One resident suggests *"they should have put older people higher up"*. Such was the level of confrontation that one old man eventually hit a child over the head with a walking stick and the police were called. Another comments dryly *"People think they have a right to live in silence…but it's a city, not a morgue!"*

At various times, a playground on the terrace outside the Tenants and Residents' Association (TRA) room in Foundling Court had been proposed, and a drop-in based at the TRA Room. But for some families there was simply no need – not when Coram's Fields, the children's playground, lay just across the Square. And not only Coram's Fields, but Collingham Gardens, St George's Gardens, Brunswick Square, and Russell Square, which all offered easily accessible play areas.

Disputes over the use of the terraces for any kind of recreation continue into the present, as Allied London repaves and replants them, with no prospect of the spaces having any real purpose except to guarantee the privacy of residents. Even the possibility of new seating there sets alarm bells ringing with many residents, who are convinced they will merely provide a magnet for antisocial behaviour, as they did in the past. In 2004, Stuart Tappin and his partner Isabelle Chaise managed to secure a Groundworks grant for a consultative project to investigate a possible future use. Local architect Rob Bishop was invited to coordinate workshops with residents to explore their ideas about the place. Some fun was had, especially by local children, planting large temporary garden boxes, but ultimately the project was deemed not to be viable. Many residents felt it was impractical – the wooden boxes would rot, there would be a problem with vandalism, and nobody would take responsibility for long-term watering. The project exposed a lack of consensus rather than a lack of ambition as to the aesthetic treatment of the Brunswick. One resident said *"we're all in favour of having something else"*, and described a vivid vision of fountains, lights and mirrors on the terraces, but was adamant that whatever was done must be easy to maintain and not provide any kind of invitation to children to play there. For, she explained, when people come home at the end of day, the last thing they want is noise outside their windows.

Tappin and Chaise had already had some experience of organising a large-scale intervention at the Brunswick with their Art Project the previous year. It was described[9] in the *Camden Chronicle*, under the headline 'Bizarre art bid to stop "neglect" of Brunswick Centre', as a *"cutting-edge art show organised by residents of the Brunswick Centre in Marchmont Street, Somers Town"*, apparently relocating the Brunswick north of the Euston Road. The installations, commissioned from 19 artists, included, besides that shown in [45], a giant curtain hung within the Brunswick Square loggia, projections of residents' wallpaper on the exterior of the building, and a pack of life-size replica Dalmatians burying their heads in the concrete on the terraces. The intent was to draw public attention to the Brunswick as 'one of London's

9 *Camden Chronicle*, 20 March 2003, p 3.

best-known buildings', and, in Chaise's words, to its incredible potential, despite being tragically neglected by the Council and the freeholder.

According to Chaise, the exhibition was not particularly well received by residents. By contrast, she suggested, other estates, such as the nearby Hillview Estate (an 1890s estate of brick-built blocks around courtyards in King's Cross) were more proactive.

> *"There's a much better atmosphere, they organise...a kind of fiesta in the summer with their neighbours, doing gigs and things, involving children, it's much more celebrated."*

The Brunswick, perhaps, with its large complement of sheltered housing, could never be quite like that, and the emphasis seems always to have been on maintaining peace and quiet, privacy, and a degree of anonymity for its residents.

There is just one modest, officially designated community space at the Brunswick: the small TRA room on the podium level. Recent rumours of a possible new community centre on top of the new supermarket were quickly quashed by those who questioned the need for any such facility. The TRA Room is used for Tenants and Residents' Association meetings, occasional children's parties and other low-key social events and, more regularly, on a Sunday by an African church congregation who, by all accounts, raise the roof with their choral singing. This is bluntly described by one resident as 'an awful noise', and clearly passes the bounds of what is considered acceptable to fellow residents. Perhaps this expresses a typically English attitude to privacy: as one observer comments, the same building relocated to Naples would be used in a completely different way, people calling out to neighbours from one side to the other, the whole place festooned with washing, alive with sound and activity.

For one source inside the building, the censorious attitude of neighbours towards local disturbances can be oppressive. She describes the Brunswick as *"a very isolating building, the most unfriendly place I have ever lived in"*, yet at the same time *"most of the people in it are actually very sociable"*. Nobody ever throws a party here, she says, because the noise generated by objectors is likely to be greater than that of the party itself; yet the funeral of an elderly neighbour was the occasion for a stream of visitors to the flat, evidence of the strength of social networks locally. She believes that much of the problem stems from the design of the building, which doesn't provide workable social spaces for people to meet and interact. As a result,

> *"we don't use a large part of our built environment or only do so in a restricted manner, so it's no surprise that people are generally very quiet here."*

Comments such as these challenge the condescending opinions published in the specialist architectural press more than once, along the lines that council tenants

> *"would be unlikely to be respectors [sic] of the clean contemporary lines of the exterior"* [10]

or again

> *"The inhabitants of the Brunswick had little choice, and their preferred lifestyle would probably be suburban."* [11]

---

10 Murray, Peter (1971) *Architectural Design* (Oct). Academy Editions, London.
11 Knight, Christopher (1993). 'Blast Brunswick'. Letters, *Building Design* 26 Nov, quoting his own article in *Building Design* in 1978.

The reality is that the residential community at the Brunswick is immensely varied in background, education, ethnicity, and aspiration – from the elderly 'twin-set and pearl set', as one source puts it, to local Holborn families, 'young professionals', academics, Spanish, Cantonese, Afro-Caribbean, Ghanaian, Bengali, central and eastern European immigrants, as well as Italian immigrants with connections to the long-standing local Italian community. A significant proportion of the able-bodied residents work in the various local hospitals, academic and educational institutions, hotels, restaurants, retail outlets, and Council offices, with increasing numbers of architects, artists, journalists and other 'creative' types working from home. Residents who are retired or suffering ill-health may inhabit the sheltered flats. It is impossible to generalise about the desires and aspirations of such a wide range of people. Although no doubt many residents *"hate the A-frame, dream of living in a brick house and of having proper windows"*, many others are intent on staying at the Brunswick. Both the failings of the building as a social vehicle, as well its more positive features, are experienced in much the same way by all those who live here, notwithstanding differences in education, affluence, or taste.

'The two estates'

One factor has a significant impact on patterns of sociability within the building: what has been called the 'fight-back' against the developers, which has on the one hand created a sense of real community through the perceived injustices of the freeholder, but on the other revealed a division of the community across clearly defined lines: the lateral boundaries of Foundling and O'Donnell Courts. Residents of Foundling Court asked why support should be given to O'Donnell Court over the 'lean-to' building when O'Donnell had not supported Foundling in an earlier battle to stop the hotel to the west from building additional storeys that block the light. One observer refers to O'Donnell and Foundling Courts as 'the two estates', suggesting that the Brunswick is a less united community than it might be.

In the original scheme [46], the continuity of the terraces around the roof of the shopping hall was to have created a sense of unity between the two buildings, but only a limited connecting area was built, and this was removed in the mid-1990s along with the grand staircase and the narrow footbridges connecting the two sides.

"It's often a nuisance to walk round to cross from one side of the flats to the other, so I use the second floor",

said one tenant before the footbridges were removed on the advice of the police, and against the wishes of most residents. Furthermore, Foundling Court has immediate access to the shops of Marchmont Street, whereas residents of O'Donnell Court must walk all round the outside. People from Foundling Court meet in Marchmont Street shops and consolidate social relationships, while O'Donnell Court addresses the less populated space of Brunswick Square. Safeway provided a useful meeting-spot between the two, not just for shopping, but also catching up on news. It remains to be seen whether the new Waitrose, which opened on 20 July 2006, will fulfil the same function.

Visions of the Brunswick

One of the short-term tenants of the retail precinct in the run-up to regeneration was Myrtle, an advertising and media agency which occupied a prominent corner site adjacent to the Renoir cinema, and stood out from the more established retail outlets around it – the launderette, local cafés, a cut-price shoe shop, charity shop and so on. The decision to locate at the Brunswick, rather than in media-friendly Soho, was made because it was

> "*somewhere that reflected the people we deal with on a daily basis, and allowed us to be in touch with a real community.*"

According to Myrtle, their clients were surprised by the location, but enjoyed it, 'watching little dramas out of the window' while at the same time, film crews would turn up to shoot other-worldly scenes for film and television, including a trailer for David Blaine's glass-box stunt under a bridge on the Thames, a Smirnoff Ice commercial, or a trailer for an American sci-fi serial.

The directors of Myrtle were not alone in regarding the Brunswick as being both everyday and "*like some giant spaceship landed in genteel Bloomsbury, really cool.*" Back in 1975, director Antonioni used the building in his film *The Passenger,* starring Maria Schneider and Jack Nicholson, moving the scene from Egypt to the Brunswick, to provide a stunning first impression of 'swinging' London. More recently, parts of Lynda LaPlante's *The Governor* series for television were shot here, and a scene for the film *Bridget Jones: the Edge of Reason*, with Renée Zellweger and Colin Firth was set outside the Renoir cinema. The BBC used the Renoir portal as backdrop for one of the dance scenes in a recent series of BBC channel 1 'idents'. Thus, the image of the Brunswick as a down-at-heel shopping precinct is negated by its evocation of a whole range of more exotic associations in the public imagination. The metaphors used to describe the Brunswick are wide and varied, and seem to provide a significant measure of its success as a building and a work of architecture in a period where the aspiration to practise architecture as a vehicle of cultural expression is increasingly derided and fast disappearing.

Will the Brunswick's special appeal to the imagination survive its regeneration as a new 'high street' for Bloomsbury? In 2005-2006, dramatic new images of the Brunswick appeared undergoing radical invasive surgery, bandaged, or under wraps. While the launch of refurbishment works awakened tremendous optimism and marked a triumphant recommencement of works prematurely halted, the patent commercial resolve to create a successful shopping 'destination' raised the possibility that, after all, an enveloping 'ordinariness' might overwhelm the more exotic aspects of the Brunswick's historic identity.

It is always traumatic to witness a building being smashed apart, even when the intention is to mend and rebuild, and the sheer force and violence involved in breaking up and removing huge sections of reinforced concrete to make way for new, comparatively lightweight structures literally made the earth shake. Shortly after work commenced, on 7 July 2005 the whole surrounding area was thrown into shock, and for a while into a deep and unnerving silence, by the explosions of two terrorist bombs nearby. At this point, the Brunswick became the focus of a new and sad attention, the background to a landscape marked by shock, loss and grief.

A year on, it is tempting to see the onward march of works at the Brunswick, the shiny painted façades rising above the surrounding streets, plus the sparkling white Chinese granite paving, as the start of a positive new era both for the building and the neighbourhood [47]. The residents went through hell with the noise, the vibrations, the grit and dust thrown up by drilling, sandblasting and repairs to the concrete, and none of them knows how much autonomy they will have over their own balcony areas – the part of the building where public most expressively meets private. In the past, residents have enjoyed it as a canvas for the display of individual tastes in colour and garden design, unfettered by council regulations, and some made the most of the opportunity to plant an individual mark on the building's public face; but such practices may take on an unprecedented subversive dimension with respect to the public image of the newly branded Brunswick. There is conflict between public and private interest in the outcry over the newly completed supermarket roof – a dramatic vertical sawtooth profile of skylights shaped like 'massive metal-clad fins' [43], which has radically altered the aspect from many flats at the north end and which is widely considered as unacceptable as unexpected. There is talk of compensation for residents, and bitter criticism of the freeholder for refusing to paint the internal walkways that are not seen by the public at large. And there is promise of further confrontation and disruption to come, with the re-emergence of discussions about a possible future vertical extension of the Brunswick, to provide an additional storey of private penthouse flats. Whatever the outcome, though, one thing seems clear: the Brunswick has a fresh lease of life ahead of it, and while it may not be a phoenix rising from the ashes, it will certainly be a new animal. It may not be to everyone's liking, but it shows that the Brunswick has an inherent vitality and resilience which have allowed it to be re-programmed in response to social change in a positive and optimistic way.

[1] Two houses in Marchmont Street, 1903; like most, the ground floor housed a shop. In 1903 there were at least three butchers in Marchmont Street, one of which evidently survived until the 1960s according to the quotation on p 9.

[2] Run-down houses in Brunswick Square in the 1950s.

[3] A sparkling new Brunswick Centre seen from the east (corner of Brunswick Square and Bernard Street) soon after construction.

[4] O'Donnell Court seen from the west, showing the famous terraces with their 'winter gardens'.

[5] Looking (c.1972) from Brunswick Square through the portico to the monumental flight of steps connecting the terrace level to the podium. (Staircase later demolished.)

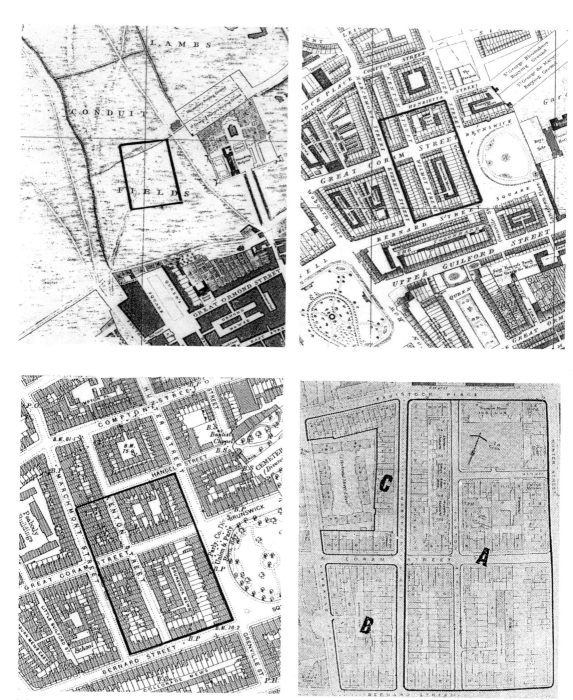

[6] Maps of the Foundling Estate, showing the Brunswick site. *Top left* c.1745, *top right* c.1813, *bottom left* 1894, *bottom right* 1952. Outlined area on first three maps corresponds to Site A, allocated for housing and complementary uses by Alec Coleman, as shown in 1952 map. Site B was allocated for offices and commercial use, and Site C for future housing.

[7] Lewis Mumford's Superblock concept, illustrated by the Ten Eyck Houses in the Williamsburg district of Brooklyn (before 1938).

[8] Charles Holden's 'spinal scheme' for development northward from Senate House, University of London (early 1930s).

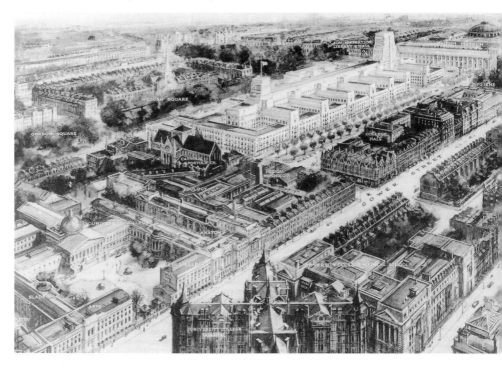

[9] Cut-away perspective of the Leslie Martin/Patrick Hodgkinson outline planning scheme (1960-63), before the introduction of the A-frame structure and shopping hall, and showing the circular recital hall in the centre.

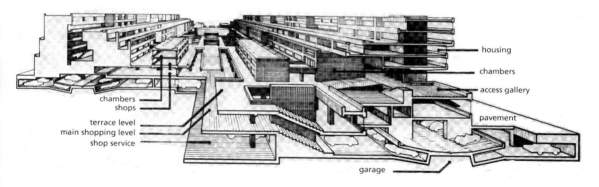

housing

chambers

access gallery

chambers
shops

pavement

terrace level
main shopping level
shop service

garage

[10] Harvey Court, 1957-62: student accommodation designed for Gonville and Caius College, Cambridge, by Patrick Hodgkinson with Leslie Martin. Note the stepped profile and internal courtyard.

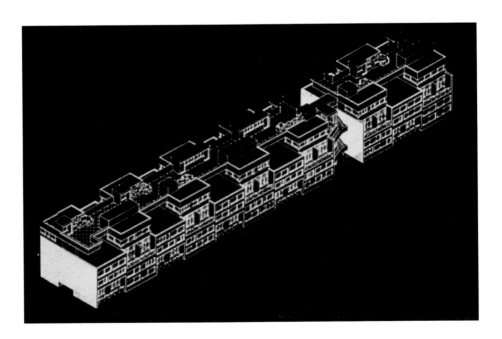

[11] Patrick Hodgkinson's housing scheme for Loughborough Estate, Brixton: student redesign (1953) of the LCC's housing estate, with low-rise, linear terraces enclosing garden courts.

[12] Le Corbusier's Unité d'Habitation, Marseilles, 1952. Hodgkinson found it 'an impenetrable slab'.

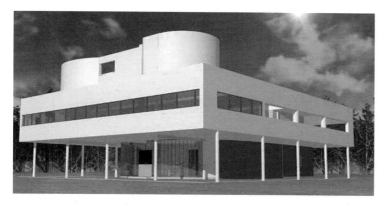

[13] Le Corbusier's Villa Savoye, Poissy, France, 1931. Hodgkinson found 'nothing existential' about it.

[14] Pierre Chareau's Maison de Verre, Paris 1932. Jean-Paul Sartre described it as 'existential' architecture.

[15] Le Corbusier's concept for a 'Ville Radieuse', showing slab blocks in open spaces, the exact opposite of the Brunswick.

Comparisons and contrasts with Brunswick design.

[16] Design for transport interchange (Sant'Elia 1914). Hodgkinson points out that the Brunswick loggia, which came to resemble it, was originally conceived as part of a long arcaded cornice fronting Brunswick Square ([17], below, which was part of the scheme approved by the council, but never built.

[18] Moshe Safdie's housing scheme, Montreal (1967), 'concerned with solidity rather than the enclosure and definition of void'.

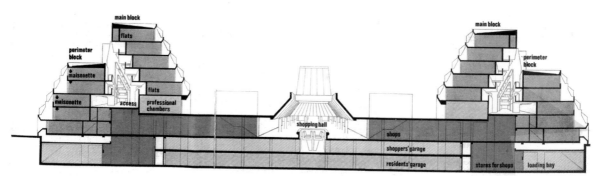

[19] West-east section of Brunswick design showing the housing piled in stepped sections above terrace level on either side, professional chambers opening onto the terraces, shopping hall with raised glass roof, and two basement levels of car parking and service access.

[20] Apartment block (1911) by Henri Sauvage at 26 rue Vavin, Paris. The terraced façade was one of various sources of inspiration behind the design of the Brunswick.

[21] Hodgkinson's early concepts for the Brunswick explored the possibility of a 'grid of Harvey Courts' covering the site like a blanket (*left*). This layout evolved into one of blocks wrapping around courtyards, with a central street down the middle (*right*).

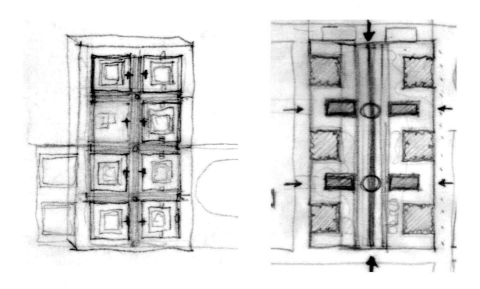

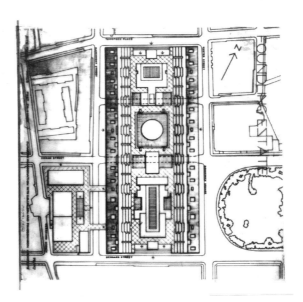

[22] Outline planning scheme for the Brunswick showing a more formal concept focused on a circular recital hall at the intersection of north-south and east-west axes, subsequently replaced by a cinema located under the loggia, now the Renoir arts cinema.

[23] The original speculative flat plans show a T-shaped living-room/kitchen with bedrooms opening directly off the living-space, and a winter-garden extending the whole length of the flat. *From left to right*: studio flat, one-bedroom flat, two-bedroom flat, three-bedroom flat, with en-suite bathrooms/shower-rooms and separate, but connecting, WCs.

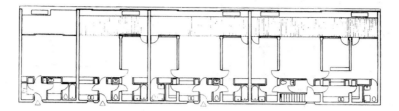

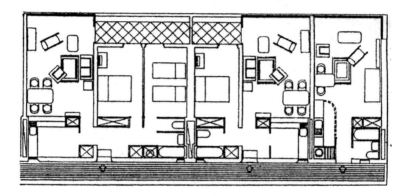

[24] Plans of flats as built for the Council. Three-bedroom flats have been banished and plans for the smaller flats has become more cellular. The wintergardens have been replaced by balconies. Studio flat on the right.

[25] Richard Buckminster Fuller's Dymaxion House (1929) was a model of innovative thinking around housing design and the use of prefabricated elements.

[27] (above) Le Corbusier's housing scheme (1931) at Fort l'Empereur in Algiers.

[26] (left) Neave Brown's Alexandra Road housing, 1972-8, commissioned by the London Borough of Camden.

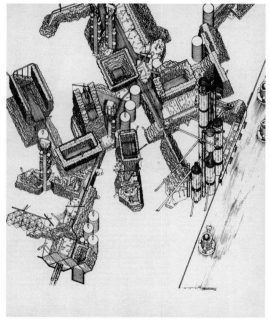

[28] (above) Archigram's design for a Plug-In City (1964).

[29] (left) Paul Rudolph's Lower Manhattan Expressway Project (1970) proposing monumental 'Terrassenhäuser' bridging major traffic arteries.

Some civic 'megastructures' built after World War II

[30] L Hugh Wilson and Geoffrey Copcut's Cumbernauld Town Centre, 1960

[31] Roger Harrison (New Town Corporation)'s Runcorn Shopping Centre (1967)

[32] Ralph Erskine's Byker Wall, Newcastle (1968)

[33] Chamberlain Powell and Bonn's Barbican Centre, London (designed 1956, flats completed 1975, arts centre in 1982)

Two buildings by Denys Lasdun

[35] (right) Student accommodation at the University of East Anglia (1963) influenced by Hodgkinson's Harvey Court (Fig 10, p 82).

[34] (below) London University's Institute of Education (1977) was, Lasdun said, 'cribbed' from the Brunswick.

[36] St George's Fields, Marylebone, a 'mini-megastructure' (Design 5, 1974).

[37] An example of British Brutalism: Hunstanton School (Alison and Peter Smithson 1954).

Unsuccessful redevelopment schemes

[38] View from Bernard Street of scheme by Le Riche Maw (1992) for Tranmac, with 7-storey, brick-built structure in a pastiche traditional style; a further block was proposed within the Renoir portico.

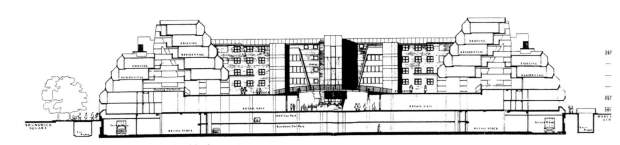

[39] David Rock/Camp 5 scheme (1993) proposing a 12-storey block of flats in front of the Renoir portico.

More unbuilt redevelopment schemes

[40] Aerial perspective of Hawkins Brown/Michael Squire scheme (1996), with new housing block filling the Brunswick Square loggia and alterations to the shopping precinct including forward extension of the supermarket into the public space.

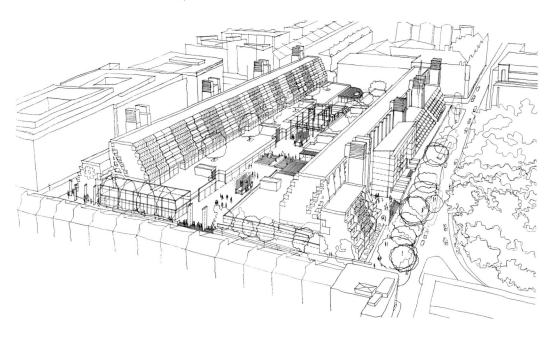

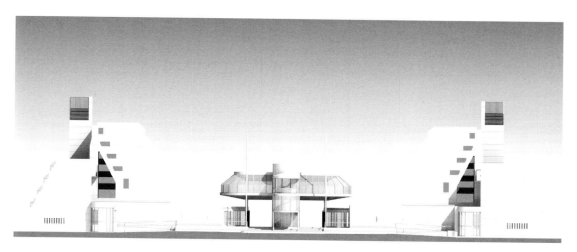

[41] West-east section through Stubbs Rich scheme (1999, commissioned by Allied London), with centrally positioned glazed restaurant structure.

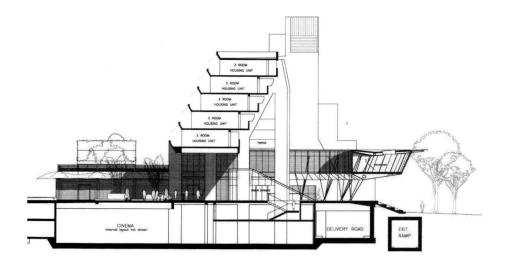

Section through the Brunswick loggia showing a proposed elevated glazed restaurant projecting towards Brunswick Square to act as an 'eye-catcher' to attract visitors to the building from the east.

Drawing of this feature, which was *not* included in the first phase of building works completed September 2006, but still has planning permission

Perspective from Bernard Street through the shopping precinct to the new supermarket building closing the north end; new canopies over new shop façades on either side of public space.

Perspective from the north-east along Handel Street including the north entrance to the supermarket and Foundling Court beyond it.

[43] Inside some Brunswick flats looking out (including, bottom right, intrusive new sawtooth roof of supermarket).

[45] Installation by Arkem, one of 19 artworks commissioned as part of the Brunswick Art Project (2003), organised by Isabelle Chaise and Stuart Tappin.

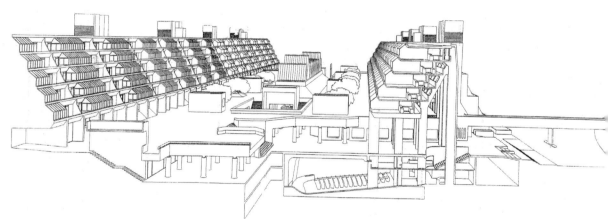

[46] Cut-away perspective, looking north, of original speculative scheme, showing how the terraces connect around the shopping hall roof, and the important role of the external staircase, now demolished, in connecting the ground and podium levels.

[47] Views of the refurbished Brunswick, 2006. Above, external façades. Below, the new shopping precinct, showing gleaming white canopies over shop fronts, and the prominent rectangular surround to the new supermarket at the north end.

Index

(* = illustration)